Nathan

He would be somebody...
it was just a matter of time.

Nathan Ballard
with Michael Rogers

RBC Publishing
Elk Grove, California

ISBN 0–9703178–0–8

Library of Congress Card Number 00-191521

Contents

Acknowledgments

God the Almighty &
Jesus Christ
Maya Angelou
Miho Azuma
Ada Mae Ballard
Carter Beauford
Hunter Bell
Jonathan Bogardus
Earnestine Calhoun
Carey C. Carlan
Jimmy Carter
Nikki Clark-Brown
Stacey Lynn Cohen
Victor & Mickey
Cohen
Vern Collins
Betty Crowley
Melissa Dalton
Mary Dates
Shedric Davis
Tom Davis
Mary Jo Deaver
Al Dupont
Melissa Foley
Sam Forkner
Dr. Rose Gladney
Bert Guy
Griffith Harsh
Josh Hinds
Dr. Loretta Holder
Byron Houston
Annie Bell Jackson
Daniel Kebede
Jim Kellen
Tony Kirchman
Dr. Harry Knopke
Connie Lee-Swope
Steven Wesley Lytton
Michael MacDonald
Jane Maples
Jeff Marshall
Buddy Mason
Dr. David Mathews
Dave Matthews
Gian Metzger
Fannie Miles
Johnny Nash
Sherry Lynn O'Brien
Partners in
Policymaking
Mariana Pernia
Gene Poole
Betsy Prince
Daryl Rayburn
Rowena Rhodes
Bettye Roberts
Rick Roden
Augie & Mabel Rogers
Charles & Patrick
Rogers
Jerry Rosenberg
Dr. Roger Sayers
Gil Scott-Heron
Dr. Amilcar Shabazz
Bernie Sloan
Ted Springfield
Stewart Stevenson
Joyce Taylor
T. J. Boyd Tinsley
Berkhan Tosyiali
John Paul Weber
Dan Wilson
Jill Lynette Yellock

In Memory of:

Ada Mae Ballard, Nora Lee Jackson,

Milton Ballard, Glori Rogers and Jim Travis.

I lovingly dedicate this book to

my niece, Nicole Danielle Brown Clark,

and my beautiful Bernice Ryans,

who will always be in my heart.

Foreword

We are lucky in life if we come across someone like Nathan Ballard. Even meeting him on these pages will be a pleasure. Nathan would be the last person to say he is a saint, but he is a genuine article. He writes what he hears, sees, and feels just the way he hears, sees, and feels it—without apology.

If there is any exaggeration, it is that he gives too much credit to his friends.

It stretches the fact to say that I was responsible for the federal legislation Nathan attributes to me. The fact is that most of what Nathan has accomplished has been accomplished because of incredible inner strengths of determination and resilience. He has had to master a body that fights his every impulse. His bouts with depression have literally been life-and-death struggles. Despite it all, he has grown into a bright, charming, and accomplished young man.

Some people are self-made. Nathan is more. He is one of a few people I've known who have invented themselves. Of course he benefited from a loving family, good friends, and dedicated counselors, but he had no role model. Nathan's greatest accomplishment is Nathan. No one could cure his cerebral palsy; still, Nathan has done what physicians cannot do—he has healed himself. In the best sense of the word "healing," he has made himself whole.

Nathan is not an end unto himself, however. He has never taken more than he has given in return. Ask the people who have known him. In this book, Nathan celebrates life—not just his life, but life itself. For example, I have never seen anybody as excited about learning as he was when Nathan began taking what most students regard as routine freshman courses. More than in the classroom, Nathan learns from living. His enthusiasm for that learning is infectious. He celebrates what he has learned and, in this book, he invites you to share in his celebration.

David Mathews, President
The Kettering Foundation

Preface

In an increasingly complicated world, I have learned the value of simple faith. The experience I have had writing this story with Nathan Ballard is immeasurable and inexplicably wonderful. He has been my friend and cohort over the past seven years, and the kinship we share is beyond description. He knows what time it is, and that's all that matters. If he inspires you to reevaluate your relationship with yourself and others, then his spirit will remain in your heart and mind as it has in the lives of every contributor to his text. Countless others have been in some way touched by this man and have had the privilege of his acquaintance.

For those who have not yet experienced his rich humor, striking intensity, and depth of feeling, this book represents my best efforts at tying together a project spanning the full length of twenty years. The life and lessons of Nathan Ballard hold powerful wisdom. Truly, this man knows the genuine ecstasy of sheer living and the agony of a depth I cannot begin to fathom. Despite disabilities, triumphs, and tragedies, he thrives and shares his knowledge with anyone willing to lend a patient and friendly ear. Occasionally, our teamwork sheds insight of its own. Absorb, weigh, compare, ponder, feel free to disagree, and approximate the good word.

Michael Rogers

PART ONE

The Early Years

Underneath the Cherry Tree

It was early spring, about March or April. There was a kind of freshness in the air and the gentle odor of honeysuckle, the singing birds, and warm sunshine filled me with a sense of wonder as we sat under the comforting branches of that old cherry tree. Uncle Nora returned with the lemonade and, brushing the area free of debris, found a comfortable spot beside me. We sat awhile in silence, mulling over our own thoughts and curiosities, watching my two younger brothers playing games in a nearby field with other neighborhood children.

"Unc . . . Uncle Nora, I wish I could play like dey can."

"Nate, I done tol' you dat God has somp'm greater for you to do."

"Uncle, what do you mean by dat?"

"You know yo' Bible, Nate?"

"Not very well."

"Lemme tell you de story 'bout Sampson an' de temple."

We would rhapsodize for hours. He illustrated how Biblical lessons could become an instrument of change for me if I'd learn to do three basic things: Listen, learn to be more patient, and believe in myself. He said, "Nate, it don't matter if you're a cripple or not, God can change you."

"Unc . . . Uncle . . . I don't undestan' . . . what you talkin' about?"

"It is not for you to undestan', not right now, but you will undestan' it later on."

As years passed, I came to see the wisdom of those talks we shared. A strong bond existed between Nora and me. He arose from family legend to become the father I never had. You see, before Uncle Nora came home, my life was one of helplessness. I knew of no outlet with which to express my creativity, and no one who believed that inside my crippled body lay the inquisitive and innocent mind of a child. No one, that is, except for my Aunt Annie Bell.

It was in December, 1954, that Aunt Annie Bell came home to West Alabama from Pennsylvania, where she worked in a mushroom factory, to spend Christmas with the family. She had previously received word by mail that there was a new addition to the household. On Wednesday, June 2, her sister Ada Mae had given birth. Her son, Nathan, had no father, being born out of wedlock. Annie Bell was overjoyed to be back in Northport where she could see the baby and visit her husband Nora, who was committed to the VA hospital in Tuskeegee.

Annie Bell hurried up the steps to our three-room shotgun house and came in out of the icy wind. Upon observing the infant she immediately remarked, "Dis here ain't no normal child. Nathan is handicapped, he ain't got enough motion fo' a baby his age."

"Ain't nuthin' wrong with him!"

"Yes dey is, Ada Mae. He don't kick an' go on like he 'spose to. Nathan is an orthopedic."

No one believed Annie Bell initially. A week passed. Others in the family noticed that, unlike other babies, I did not sit up, play with toys, focus on or grasp at objects. Another aunt, Joyce Moore, was the first to notice my strange jerking arm and leg movements.

One morning the following week, I awoke with a high fever. My mother and aunts bundled me up and carried me to Dr. Sam Davis at the Tuscaloosa Health Clinic. His preliminary diagnosis was polio, but Dr. Davis was far from certain. Once my fever responded to medication, he knew my condition was something else entirely. After three months of testing, he sent us to Crippled Children's Services (CCS) in Birmingham for further evaluation.

Momma worked hard to support the family. At this time and during the full nine months of her pregnancy she was employed as a janitor, eventually earning a promotion to cook with a significant raise, at Northport Junior High. My father, still loitering around town, took a vague interest in the situation once word got around to him, dropping off a silver dollar for me I still have today, but that was all. Momma took a day off from work, and together we rode a Greyhound into the big city. It was a doctor at CCS by the name of Simpson who solved the mystery. "Ms. Ballard, your son has a condition known as cerebral palsy. He is going to require special treatment. Please bring Nathan here again in about two weeks."

This did not go over well at home, as I'm sure you can imagine. They were all scared to death. Cerebral palsy was a condition just coming under medical scrutiny. It was virtually unknown to and unidentifiable by the public back then. No one in the family knew what to think, or whom to fault. Momma went through a period of intense denial and blamed herself. Back at CCS she learned the truth.

Cerebral palsy occurs when the brain does not get adequate oxygen during the birth process. This phenomenon is called "fetal toxemia." It has a hereditary aspect, and runs in many black families, I have discovered, though not every baby who experiences fetal toxemia develops cerebral palsy. It remains a partial mystery, even today.

A common side effect of my condition is mental retardation, and though I suffer from various afflictions I am lucky to have all my mental faculties intact. My central nervous system and cerebral cortex, the part of the brain controlling bodily movement, however, were somehow damaged at my birth. The team at CCS discovered that I have three of five types of cerebral palsy, each with its own distinctive characteristics. Tremors make me shake excessively, spastic diplegia stiffens my muscles, and athetosis creates involuntary movement throughout my body.

I do not like to speculate as to what caused my condition, because it's not moral to place blame on anyone or anything in particular. Today, I feel my condition is an asset to me rather than a liability. That's right. Cerebral palsy is just one of my many gifts from God. It has allowed me to become more aware of myself and to broaden the horizons of others. In the words of William Shakespeare, "To be, or not to be: that is the question." Remember, "There are more things in Heaven and Earth . . . than are dreamt of in your philosophy."

Steel Legs

A local taxi driver, an older black man, used to pick Momma and me up from the bus station once a month and carry us over to CCS on the corner of 18th Street and 20th Avenue. For the first eighteen months after that fateful diagnosis, Dr. Simpson worked with a pioneer team of specialists to research my condition. In 1955 they were just experimenting on people to find the most effective means of accommodating children born with cerebral palsy. I was placed on drug therapy at a very young age. From my first pharmaceutical experiences I learned that although drug therapy can placate some symptoms, it isn't a panacea for cerebral palsy. I had little control over this part of my treatment and less over my leg bracing.

I don't remember the exact date or how it began. The only thing I recall from my early bracing experience is excruciating pain. They weighed about ten pounds, consisting of hip, knee, and thigh cuffs bolted onto steel strips which were interconnected to run parallel down either side of my legs, bolting onto black, high-top orthopedic shoes. They bent at the knee to allow retraction into a sitting position. When Momma and my older brother Sam used to lock them, it felt as if I was being stretched out on a rack, with my limbs pulled in unnatural positions.

Though I had great difficulty expressing myself, Sam and I were very close, and I know in my heart he did not like to see me suffer as I did. Imagine how you would feel torturing your own brother at the instruction of doctors for reasons beyond your full understanding. Yet, these were early procedures, and, in the long run, trial-and-error has greatly improved the knowledge base. Today, with people like Gene Stallings working to generate awareness within our community of how valuable our dollars are when spent in support of programs in Tuscaloosa like Rural Infant Stimulation Environment (RISE), infants in West Alabama with developmental disabilities can receive care with the most advanced techniques available in the United States to assist them in developing toward a more fulfilling life.

Ideally, treatment begun at the earliest stages of life will decrease the special needs of these beautiful children later on. RISE is one of those long-term projects, developed by citizens with enough vision, that invest wisely in the immediate situation toward a brighter, less costly, and more independent future for people like me. It was developed through research conducted at the University of Alabama and will insure that no other child with cerebral palsy undergoes the torture I did in those braces.

At the onset, the agony was unbearable. I felt my muscles tearing and ligaments being ripped apart while my bones seemed to break. As the preliminary pain subsided, a dulling, numb, and lifeless ache pervaded my total existence. At times, I wanted to stop the world and get off.

As I began to kick and scream violently, Sam positioned each brace one at a time, by lifting my leg and placing cuffs under my upper thigh, knee, and lower thigh in succession. Entry of each foot into its orthopedic shoe required a great deal of patience because my deformed toes began to claw automatically. My feet arched and became hardened like glass. The harder Sam worked to force them into position, the more rigid my body became. The braces could not be locked until both feet were tightly laced into their respective shoes.

Once my feet were properly placed, the tongues of each shoe were straightened and pulled for lacing. As the laces were threaded and tightened, a greater anguish began. My legs were forced into an extended or straight position so the brace joints could be locked and secured. Being forced to remain in a straight position was definitely more uncomfortable than when the brace joints were released and I was put in a sitting position. Once the braces were removed, my legs were exercised—which, due to their exceptional stiffness, proved to be quite difficult.

As I had no muscle control, my legs involuntarily pitched against the metal in an attempt to scissor, causing severe bruises along my inner legs. With each passing day the skin underneath each leg would wear down and begin to break. When the bloodshed became too profuse, I was given a rest from the daily routine until my skin had enough time to heal. Then everything would begin anew.

"Momma I hate 'em. Take 'em off. Take 'em off now!"

"I can't do dat son."

"But dey hurt, dey hurt me real bad."

"Nate, de braces is fo' your own good. I'm jus' doin' what de doctor tol' me to."

"Why M . . . Momma, why d . . . do I have to wear 'em anyway?"

"'Cause someday, with de grace of God, you will be able to walk."

Walk! I believed this with my heart and soul. Rugged determination fired by my desire to be "normal" helped me through that time. I remained in braces for eight years.

One day during that first painful year, Momma brought a blue pedal car home from the store and placed me inside it on the floor. I was thrilled to death! The pedal car was my first introduction to self-propelled locomotion. I would kick my legs out in front of me, thereby propelling me backwards around the room. A few years later, around the age of five, my uncle Samuel brought home a Christmas gift that served as the vehicle for the formation of my early creative mind, a little red rocking chair.

Picture a little boy, about five or six years old. It's summertime, and the little dirt road alongside the house is alive with activity. He is sitting on the porch of his rundown shotgun house, and he is rocking, rocking his little head off, despite the crying of his newborn baby brother from inside. This little boy is encumbered by two oversized metal braces, but for the time being, they don't seem to bother him much. Beside him is a box about four feet high, which appears to serve some sort of therapeutic purpose. He doesn't take notice of the strange contraption. His mind is on other things.

There is a flurry of activity in the field ahead. It's a musty and sweltering July afternoon. Children are playing hopscotch, marbles, jacks, baseball, jump rope, and a variety of other games. As the young boy continues to rock back and forth in his chair, sweat stinging his eyes and clouding his vision, his level of agitation increases. He is consumed with the desire to be out playing with the other children, but knowing he cannot, smiles to himself and begins to devise his own games. . . .

Suddenly his chair shoots up, ascending skyward toward the stars! He is piloting his little chair-turned-spaceship to the moon and beyond. Captain Nathan Ballard is in search of other planets where perhaps more beings exist like himself. Maybe, just maybe, he will uncover a land of equals where he can find friends. But no; not today, it seems, as he is running out of fuel. The young captain must return to his landing pad/front porch and report his findings to the Earth. . . .

I created an active and detailed fantasy world. After all, who wants to run and play baseball when you can soar to the outer reaches of the universe? Over time, I invented complicated mind games: grouping numbers and colors, guessing when which leaves would turn what color, then fall first from the cherry tree's branches; anything to take my mind off the braces and the reality of my disability.

Although these games were captivating, they were further limited by an inability to coherently use my developing voice. I would also be challenged by a curious speech impediment consisting of a stutter combined with a piercing tonal quality that affects my speech even today. Doctors think this is the result of immature development of my vocal chords due to cerebral palsy. A long period of fever above one hundred degrees, during a bout with measles around my fourth year, may also be to blame. My speaking difficulties were incredibly frustrating, especially when situations arose where words became invaluable.

I remember clearly a rainy night in early January of 1960. Sam was working for a local drugstore as a delivery boy. He always brought me home a bag of Frito-Lay corn chips or a Baby Ruth candy bar when he got off work. Sometimes he would borrow the store's motorcycle on weekends to take my younger brothers and me for a ride. I remember how proud and special I felt when he would secure me on the bike and together we would race out of town and into the country. That night there was an unusually violent storm. Lightning, howling wind, and blinding rain had driven my whole family inside the house. It was a little after 7:30 p.m. and Sam was late, strangely perplexing for my punctual older brother.

There came a knock on the door. I was sitting in another room by the gas heater, waiting anxiously for my brother to bring my nightly treat, but he never arrived.

"Ada!! Ada!! Ada!!"

"Joyce, what chou doin' here?"

"Ada Mae, Sam done been in a accident! We got to git to de hospital right away!"

"Y'all take care a Nathan!"

They ran out the door together, leaving us in an acute state of shock. Rushing into the emergency room, Momma nervously awaited word from the attending physician.

"Ms. Ballard, Sam is in critical condition. We do not expect him to pull through the night. His jaw and head are seriously damaged. His throat has collapsed, and we had to perform a tracheotomy for him to breathe."

"Please . . . y'all save my boy. Save my boy."

When Momma was finally allowed to see Sam, he was covered in blood, mangled and unconscious. That was the longest night of my mother's life. He remained in a coma for twenty-one days, during which Momma stayed by his side. The few times a day she was at home, I found it nearly impossible to get her to listen for the length of time it took me to articulate a single sentence. It was a scary time for us all.

I saw Sam for the first time since that terrible night six weeks later, and he was a changed man. Though his wounds were actually life-threatening and his chances of living slim to none, Sam knew he had somehow survived. Left with impaired vision and a distinctive limp, his comprehension of my condition was greatly enhanced. Before the accident Sam viewed me sympathetically, as a burden; but after being thrust into my shoes briefly, he realized this was not the case at all. Though I felt unable to adequately express love and concern for him, Sam intimately understood.

All therapy during the years before my ninth birthday was geared toward the objective goal of walking. The lengths I went to and the continual discomfort I endured in pursuit of this dream are mind-boggling to me today. I was six years old and in my fourth year of treatment when Dr. Simpson prescribed a standing box for me to use in conjunction with the braces. A local carpenter was commissioned to build it according to Simpson's design.

The standing box was placed on the porch near my rocking chair. While in braces, if I wasn't in the rocking chair, I was inside the box, forced into an awkward and painful position. For two to three hours a day, seven days a week, I would endure the injury caused by being in an upright position while my legs were spasming inside those braces. More than anything else in the world I wanted to have my legs, and no pain was too great to jeopardize that. According to Dr. Simpson, the box led up to my last step before walking, the parallel bars.

The Ordeal

I was the happiest boy in Northport, Alabama, one hot July day back in 1963, when Dr. Simpson sent Momma and me home with a long, narrow box labeled "Parallel Bars." In this box, I thought to find the answer to my wildest dream. During the bus ride home, I had visions of playing, running, jumping up and down, and wrestling with my younger brother, Milton. He was about seven years old at the time and already held a position of authority among his peers.

I was just beginning to feel the isolating effects of peer pressure for a multiply disabled child, and gaining a grasp of what it means to be peculiar. Now, more than ever before, it was crucial that I rededicate myself to my goal. "Within a year," I swore under my breath as familiar hometown signs passed by the window, "Nathan Ballard, you will walk."

Returning home, Sam took on the task of assembling the parallel bars in the yard while I watched in feverish anticipation. There was a board about three inches thick and six by three feet wide. The bars were steel, about five pounds a piece, with fittings for each end which had to be nailed down securely to the board below. Once the bars were assembled, I fidgeted anxiously, waiting for the opportunity to try them out. Sam went inside to get Momma as I yelled from the porch, more excited than I had ever been before.

"Ma! Momma! I got these parallel bars together. Do you want to put Nathan on them now?"

"No, I got to finish cookin' first."

"I . . . I got to git myself up dere right now Sam!"

"Boy, Momma done tol' you dat you ain't gettin' up there yet."

"Momma, Momma! I . . . want . . . I want to git up dere . . . RIGHT NOW!!"

"Nate, I don't want to bust you upside your head, but you keep on and dat is what I got to do!"

"Damn y'all boys! Don't you see I'm in here tryin' to cook?"

She came outside and together they locked my braces, standing me up between the parallel bars. I gripped each bar tightly and locked my elbows. As soon as they were convinced of my solid hold, Momma and Sam let go. . . .

"Uh, Nate? You don't look so . . ."

"Aaaah! BAM!!!!"

I fell flat on my face, bruising myself badly on that hard board, and was knocked out cold. My legs, it turned out, weren't nearly strong enough to support my weight. I stayed unconscious for about five or ten minutes, waking up to distant neighborhood laughter with a splitting headache and an aching body. I was injured but determined not to give up.

Two to three hours a day, I practiced walking in my braces. After my toes were heavily bruised, ankles twisted, and leg muscles torn, I kept at it. As months passed, it became obvious that I would never walk upright; obvious, that is, to everyone but me. After eight months of exasperating effort, even I could recognize my dreams to walk would never be realized. Deep down in my heart I knew this to be true all along, but for the first time in my young life I was forced to admit defeat.

Dr. Simpson had something else up his sleeve. "Don't despair, Nathan. There remains a possibility that you may walk yet." He described to Momma two operations which would alleviate many symptoms related to my condition. The first was called a "bilateral hamstring release and a left gastrocnemius recession." This was to lengthen and straighten my legs and feet. The second was an "obturator neurectomy." If successful, it would bring my spastic body movements to a minimum.

Momma, uncertain about the value of surgery, considering all the pain she had watched me endure already at the behest of these specialists, reluctantly allowed the preparations to begin. She was spiritually shaken by all the commotion over her young son. How could she have known that because of the timing, I was playing a role in the treatment of my condition that was revolutionary and pioneering. Historically speaking, the American Civil Rights Movement shocking the world at this time also included disabled rights, although the struggle blacks were undergoing to simply achieve human dignity took precedence in the media.

I was admitted to Lloyd Noland Hospital in Fairfield, Alabama, on April 5, 1964. The first two procedures were on the following day. The surgery took about two hours, after which I was moved to the recovery room. When I came to, plaster casts covered each of my legs completely. A nurse wheeled me into a large ward filled with beds and cribs similar to mine. I was kept medicated most of the time, but the ward remained alive with activity to watch from my vantage point.

In spite of being cast in plaster, my legs still bolted, buckled, jumped, banged, and crashed against their confinement in an effort to scissor. My surgery did not, to my dismay, prevent the reemergence of characteristic cerebral palsy symptoms. Because each leg had to be straightened in order to set its cast, my overextended muscles continually raged out of control during the long recuperation. In spite of this highly intense pain, worse than the braces because my casts were unable to be removed, I remained optimistic. Dr. Hardy, the senior surgeon in Alabama for these types of procedures, released me on April 15, and my casts were removed about three months later.

On October 22 of that same year, I underwent my second major operation at Lloyd Noland. Already receiving physical therapy for my legs, I was back in braces and things were looking up. The second major operation was a success; no more tremors! My days of shaking were over at last.

I noticed, however, that something was wrong with my legs. They felt rubbery, weak, and were beginning to curl up into a fetal shape. Each knee independently rose toward my chest. My left foot, which had been straightened by the first operation, now looked swollen up and twisted inward. Regardless of what anyone said, I knew now my dream was foolish. I grew more and more depressed each day, all the while maintaining a smiling face for the outside world.

Since my first operation, I had been administered various types of muscle relaxants: Demerol (35 mg), Vistoril (50 mg), Atropine (gr. 1/200), and

Peminol (35 mg). I took all of these at different intervals every day to keep me as calm as possible while my legs were healing inside of their casts. Now a new drug, Valium (2.5 mg), was also introduced to my system so I could sleep better at night. I was released with prescriptions for all of the above on Halloween afternoon. How remarkably symbolic!

I have been under the thumb of medicine all of my life, and I have a few critical observations to make. Now, mind you, I am not a medical expert, but I am a medical model. Chemists spend a lot of time manipulating chemical combinations found in nature in an effort to find new ways of treating various conditions. God gave us the plants and animals. Our attempts to manipulate chemicals in place of studying what we found on the Earth has resulted in many medicines whose long-term effects often create more problems for our fragile bodies, because we cannot play God, no matter how hard we may try.

As I became more aggravated, I began to view the world in a different way, a darker way. My bracing continued, and I felt the whole affair was useless. The more dreary life became, the more escape I found in my drug schedule. Day and night gradually grew into a continual state of delirium. Here began the period in my life that I less than affectionately refer to as afflicted by "Dry Rot Syndrome."

Each exceptional child, regardless of their disability or appearance, has great potential. Excessive drug therapy, abuse, malnutrition, neglect, ridicule, or other negative aspects of his or her specific circumstances often create a lack of drive in the child. Encouragement and a supportive environment, wherein they find loved ones who refuse to lose faith in them, are crucial to each child's growth and educational development. My experience has been that without these things a child of any kind, whether disabled or not, will begin to wither up, lose interest in the experience of life enrichment, and "dry rot."

"Dry Rot Syndrome" happened to me because I defined my value by my ability to walk. I was very young, and everyone I looked up to at that time placed such emphasis on my walking that when I failed it made me feel worthless. Worthless-feeling children are all around you today, in homes and environments that fail, despite good intentions, to convince children of their tremendous importance and uniqueness, and of how special that makes them.

My postoperative checkups were routine, and though the doctors had hoped my legs would respond to normal physical duress, it was hopeless. By the time the doctors realized what I had already figured out, it was much too late. Their solace only deepened my despair. The dreams of my early childhood were shattered like fine crystal dashed against the pavement. Even the psychedelic side effects of the drugs I had been taking were changing.

There was a favorable response at first. My sedate attitude and relaxed muscles allowed caregivers easier control over this usually resistant body, but at what expense? I was given three to four different pills at a time, at different intervals during the day. My reflexes became progressively sluggish. I was unable to organize or clarify thoughts, and my behavior gradually became erratic and undependable.

Worst of all, my health was in jeopardy. I was gaining weight at a rapid rate: from ninety to one hundred fifty in the first six months, an additional fifty in the next six months, and twenty-five more pounds in the following three. My family was concerned but did nothing. The doctors, Momma hoped, knew what they were doing.

Actually, the doctors had little or no idea, as drug therapy for cerebral palsy was in its early experimental stages. Now I was a guinea pig of a different sort, and Aunt Annie Bell didn't like it one bit.

Annie Bell returned home on June 30, 1963. She had previously received a letter from her husband's hospital in Tuskeegee that Uncle Nora would soon be ready for release on a trial basis. After consultation with the doctors, who felt that it was best to keep Nora in Alabama instead of Pennsylvania, Annie Bell decided to stay for good. She was needed at home in more ways than she was aware. On a "ninety-day trial basis," she soon would have her husband back.

An Enduring Institution

"Hey dere! Hey dere pretty girl!" called a young black man from the other side of the hay pile. Annie Ballard had heard about this one. Nora Lee Jackson was his name, and he spelled trouble for any girl trying to stay in the good graces of the Lord. Of course, Annie had no way of knowing this yet. All she knew was that this young man was not worth her time. She found him quite obnoxious. The flatbed truck slowed down and stopped at the picnic ground.

"You sure is a pretty girl, Annie. You got de prettiest hair of any girl at Porter Saint Paul."

"Shush now, Nora! I'm not interested."

And she wasn't. Nora's mother, Liza, was close friends with Annie Bell's. Liza would tell Annie's momma all about the feelings which her son felt towards her daughter.

"He say he love her."

"He do? Well, Annie tell me she think he too wild fo' her, so I tol' her, 'All young people is wild.' She jus' don' undestan' yet, but she will!"

Sure enough, Annie Bell Ballard married Nora Lee Jackson in December of 1934. His flirtations finally made a positive impression on her. She decided to trust her mother's intuition. Nora was as charming as Annie Bell was a looker, and the ceremony was lovely. They moved in together with his mother until they could save enough money to rent a house. Times were tough all over. The Great Depression took its toll on Alabama and the rest of the nation. They worked hard to pay the bills; Nora delivered Orange Crush soda on a truck while Annie Bell cleaned houses. Their first two years together were happy, but relatively uneventful.

In 1936 Annie became ill. When the hospital told her they would have to remove her appendix, she hesitantly agreed to allow the operation to proceed. The procedure was a success, and she was kept for the following eleven days. Strangely enough, Nora did not visit once during her stay. She was concerned. This was not like her husband at all. The day of her release Annie caught a ride home with the combination hearse/ambulance.

Annie came up the dirt road to a shocking scene: Nora was running behind the house, and with him was another girl! Annie stumbled out of the car to yell, "You son of a . . . Fine! You wants to be wit' de womens, I'll leave you wit' 'em." She went inside, packed a small bag of belongings and had a neighbor carry her back home to her mother as an infuriated and heartbroken young lady. She gave up her job, her new house, even her faith.

As time passed, Nora attempted to regain her affections but to no avail. One day when he came calling, she asked for a divorce, but he would not give her one. Annie decided, after long sleepless nights of crying, "to go on about her business." She was a housekeeper for white families, and the people she worked for at the time felt she had a good head on her shoulders. As they learned Annie's story, her employers advised her to move up North where she could earn more money.

Annie went home that night fraught with anxiety. Should she stay or go? True enough, her life was at a standstill. There was another war on in Europe, once again involving a German tyrant, and her husband had disrespected her terribly. Annie needed to make a change in her life. There was no reason for her to put up with this kind of behavior any longer. That night she told her mother about the opportunity up North.

"Baby, you know we got a cousin in Detroit?"

"We do, Momma?"

"You kin always go up dere an' live wit' her. It'd be yo' decision anyway. Whatever you want to do, Annie Bell, I stan' by yo' side."

Annie found comfort in her mother's words, but she remained unsettled. Before lying down to sleep, she fell down on her knees and prayed to God for whatever divination He cared to enlighten her with. She prayed for strength; she prayed for courage and wisdom to make the right choices. "Please, Father, what should I do now?"

She learned through this meditation. Something in her future was somewhere other than Northport. If God had a plan for her life, part of that plan lay in Detroit, Michigan. A reborn Christian, Annie had found the bravery she was looking for. She bought a bus ticket the following morning and, a few days later, left for new horizons.

Annie spent two years in Detroit working just like before, as a housemaid and nanny. Though the money was good, she hated the fast-lane lifestyle and was not accustomed to the unfriendly, dangerous, big city attitude that seemed to envelop her. To make matters worse, she had to have an operation which did not allow her to work, and Annie was not the type of person who enjoyed being laid up in bed.

She went home to visit our family the following Christmas and asked if they wanted her to come home. Again, her mother explained, it would be her choice. Annie had a pleasant holiday. Perhaps she should return. Nora wouldn't talk to her, but maybe things could be worked out between them after all. She heard from friends that Nora missed her and he wasn't fooling around any more. Annie gave it some serious thought. If he truly loved her, she suspected, he wouldn't have cheated on her in the first place.

The damage was done. Annie was hurt, and the wounds Nora had previously inflicted on her ran deep. When the day came to disembark, she packed up her things and went down to the station. It was 1940, eight years after her marriage. She sat down on the bus next to a lady who introduced herself as Rose Hamperton. Rose hailed from Savannah, Georgia, and Annie soon knew this ride would be very interesting.

"Well, Rose, pleased to meet you. Dey call me Annie, but my name is Annie Bell."

"Visitin' yo' family?"

"Uh-huh, fo' de holiday, maybe comin' back fo' good."

"Why is dat, Annie, if'n you don't mind me askin'?"

"I live in Detroit, but it be too fast up dere fo' me. I think it's best fo' me to come on back here. I need de money, but it ain't worth it to have, if'n you ain't alive to spend it."

"What chou mean?"

"Every day people is dyin', gettin' shot up in de street. I got me a place with my cousin, but Detroit, it ain't safe, not one bit."

"Well lord no! Why, dere ain't no need fo' you to stay in Detroit, an' dere is no reason fo' you to go home."

"What are you sayin'?"

"You could always come stay wit' me."

"Where you livin' at?"

"Pennsylvania, a little town, not crazy like dat, called Chester. I got me a place with her, over dere, an' we is lookin' fo' a roommate. Annie, dis here is Tressie Graham."

And so it came to be. Annie, Rose, and Tressie hit it off, and they made plans during their long ride up north for Annie to come and live with them. Rose worked in a mushroom factory where she had met Tressie the previous year, and they were convinced that Annie should come and work there too. It was even more money than she had been making as a maid and in a safer place. She got off the bus in Detroit with newfound purpose. Within a day Annie said her good-byes, quit her job, and bought a ticket to Chester.

Her conversation with Rose and Tressie had fired up her imagination. She would start a new life in Pennsylvania, a life filled with more pleasure than pain, more hope than regret. She thanked God for bringing her together with these new friends. She knew that the Almighty must have had a hand in their chance meeting which would bring her out of her maelstrom and into more benevolent waters.

She arrived in Chester where Rose met up with her, and together they drove to the house. Kind of small, it was broken up into three separate apartments, allowing each occupant maximum privacy. Indeed, this was to Annie's satisfaction. She now had a place to examine her life in peace.

Thanks to money Annie had saved (and she was always putting money aside), the rent for her first few months was paid for in advance. Things were coming together for her, and Annie was at ease.

As soon as she was able, Annie began working at the mushroom factory. She put away everything that she made, and attended church on a regular basis. In every town she lived, in every place that she visited, Annie always found a Methodist church where she could praise God for allowing her to recognize and evaluate the evolution of her life so clearly. Today it may seem like working in a mushroom factory wouldn't be such a big deal, but in 1940 people were lucky to find work at all. Annie, as a black working woman, was making good money, exceptionally good money.

The economic situation in the United States was on the brink of another revolution. On December 7, 1941, the Japanese bombed Pearl Harbor, catapulting us into the bloodiest conflict in our world's history to date. After an emergency meeting, Congress declared war on Germany, Italy, and Japan the following day. They reinstated mandatory service, and Nora was drafted that very year.

Annie began to receive from Nora, government checks in the amount of fifty dollars a month and she deposited them in an account for him. But, it took half a year before the money began to arrive, starting with a large sum of back-owed funds from the past six months. Annie was glad to be receiving compensation, but she had not the slightest notion of the hell Nora was enduring.

The Gift

Uncle Nora and I were kindred spirits. We shared a special bond that is difficult to put into words. Born in 1914 to a family of sharecroppers, he was one of sixteen children, with eight brothers and seven sisters. Uncle Nora's childhood was tough. His brothers and sisters had to help their parents by trudging out to pick cotton with them as soon as they were old enough. Nora's father died when he was twelve years old, and the loss put a tremendous burden on the family. Those trying events taught him the importance of living one day at a time and gave him a greater appreciation of the good times that were to come.

In 1926, following the death of his father, Nora's mother decided to move to Northport, a city that was ten or so miles away from the property they worked. She wanted a better life for her children and tried to send them to school. In town there was a segregated school that black children could attend. Eventually Nora went, and he completed the fourth grade.

Nora gained a reputation to be reckoned with as a teenager. He could fistfight, charm the ladies and their parents, and used his quick wit to wreak havoc on the often-times quiet town. Nora liked to drink. He had a dislike for working and a fascination with people. Back in those days you either loved or hated my uncle.

When he met Annie Bell, Nora was twenty years old. At that point in his life, I guess you could call him "girl crazy." He had no real concept of commitment and was not mature enough to get hitched. Of course, neither one of them realized this. Their parents more or less arranged the marriage; that's the way things were done back in those days. Once she caught him cheating, and believe me, Nora was a playboy, Annie wanted nothing to do with him.

Today the divorce she wanted would be easy, but divorce is sometimes utilized as a quick way out of difficult situations. I'm not defending my uncle's behavior, just pointing out that today their marriage would be, by all accounts, considered an exemplary one. In my opinion, the ease with which married couples can get divorced has cheapened and weakened the institution. In 1936 it was nearly impossible for a woman to seek divorce without her husband's consent.

Though the circumstances were unfair for Auntie, I am glad she was unable to annul their marriage. Had she been successful, I would not have the life I live today, and they would have missed out on a beautiful relationship once the troubles were worked through and Uncle Nora matured. I remember Nora telling me that all marriages are something you work at. They are like cultivating a flourishing garden, the bad patiently weeded out so that the good can grow and blossom.

Divorce is sometimes a necessity, when the arrangement is ill-conceived, full of physical abuse or other atrocities. Marriage to another human being is the most important decision you will ever make, and those not devoting their life to a cherished agreement with their dearest confidant and friend shouldn't waste their time. My uncle taught me that being a man is more than just boasting your manhood. It is important to let your views be known before an outburst of feelings erupts in an unseemly way. Your spouse is as unique, as important, and as much a child of God as you.

I wish more couples would look to God to direct them through trials before filing paperwork, like Auntie and Uncle did, instead of making a mistake that creates double jeopardy for their children and messes up God's quiet plans for their life. I believe there is a plan for everyone, and looking for its direction kept my aunt and uncle strong through difficult and unfortunate times. Annie Bell stood by Nora during the war for reasons that are obvious today. Back then, she wasn't sure of anything but the power of prayer. She just prayed, worked, and trusted her instincts. Wait and see how much God blessed their life and marriage after all the hard work they put into gardening it!

When Nora entered into military service in 1944, he was assigned to the Army Quartermaster Corps, considered the backbone of the armed forces during World War II. His unit was in charge of all food, laundry, bedding, cleaning, provisions, and supplies. He anticipated the needs of others under continual attack on the front lines. Men commissioned to the Quartermaster Corps also assured that all the necessary preparations were made for each new battalion entering their assigned barracks.

After basic training, Nora was stationed in France. He and the troops assigned with him had to live in scattered pup tents of a supply camp about ten or fifteen miles behind the lines, sometimes closer and sometimes farther, but never far away. They were always in fear of German or Italian bombing runs. Once a plane flew overhead while he and his comrades were asleep, dropping two bombs on the campsite. They both exploded in prime areas, killing 47 men and injuring many others. Fortunately, Nora's tent was strategically placed behind a large supply truck, and he was not harmed.

Despite the danger, Nora's supply team worked on an as-needed basis, and he went on regular furlough. He enjoyed meeting new people and reaped the benefits of exploring a world he had never known. Uncle was intrigued with the variety of foreign languages he encountered, especially the musical sound of spoken French and Italian. He had a playful and roguish personality that ached for adventure and a good time. These encounters with foreign cultures fascinated Nora, but he would have traded it all to be away from the nightmare of those nights delivering supplies to the front.

The mighty Nazi Empire of Hitler's infamous design was crumbling around him as the Allied front advanced on Berlin. The Germans left the surrounding countryside a mass of burnt rubble, destroying towns and raping the land. The starving people left in ruin would scavenge food from Allied battalions. Nora had his shift of guard duty one cold November night in 1944. He was in the habit of sneaking food for those impoverished people. Nora was moved by their plight, being poor himself, and tried to help out as much as he could without risking trouble from his superiors. Carrying out some scraps of food that night, he heard a noise that sounded suspicious. Investigating the brush, Nora tripped on a wire. A gun fired, and he screamed out in agony as the bullet lodged into his leg.

When he was discovered, the camp surgeon removed the bullet and sterilized his wound with alcohol. The booby trap had evidently been left behind by the retreating Nazi army. He was lucky that the bullet, although painful, did not break his leg. No infection set in, and once released from the infirmary, Nora was placed back on active duty.

One morning about one year later, a truck transporting bombs for aerial combat approached and passed near their quarters. Boom! There was a massive explosion as the truck engulfed in flames, and jagged slivers of shrapnel came flying out in all directions. Several people outside died instantly. Nora, sheltered in a tent, was lying down talking to some men in his battalion when the accident occurred. There was a loud sound, followed by the familiar hiss of flying metal as everyone dove for cover. The shards came flying through the tent's side like tiny knives, killing some and maiming others. The last thing he remembered was a sudden, intensely sharp pain piercing his back, and then nothing.

Uncle regained consciousness at a military hospital in Frankfurt, Germany. The doctors had picked out most of the pieces, but not all. Though heavily drugged on morphine, he was made to understand they were flying him back to the United States. In New York City, there was a doctor who specialized in the type of operation required to remove a tiny sliver of metal which was lodged dangerously close to his spinal cord. Had anything hit his spinal cord directly, Nora likely would have died.

Twelve hours of grueling flight later, he was back in America. The operation that took place soon afterwards was a success. Annie Bell was informed, but for financial reasons was unable to visit him during his recovery. This was probably a good thing because Nora was deteriorating. The horror of combat, combined with this latest injury, tore his already fragile mind to pieces. Nora had become a victim of post-traumatic shock syndrome, formerly known as "shell shock," and no medicine in the world could aid him.

The doctors transferred my uncle to the infamous VA hospital in Tuskeegee, Alabama, where he was to spend the next nineteen years. Those same nineteen years would eventually bring him into my life for the first time, back into Annie Bell's arms, and to an intimate understanding of the simple beauty in life.

The Road Back

The summer of 1963 Aunt Annie Bell returned home for good. She had been accruing the financial benefits of her husband's injury. Taking that, combined with her own earnings, she opened a savings account in a Pennsylvania bank. Annie figured that the money which came from Nora's accident belonged to him. Annie and Nora had been writing back and forth since his admission to the VA hospital. Nora was ready for release on a trial basis, and Annie Bell, empowered by the forgiveness only love can engineer, decided the time had come for healing.

They already had fallen back in love again, as Nora came to the realization that he needed her. Not only that, he wanted to share a life with her forever and express the newfound pure joy that each day filled him with. My uncle had undergone a metamorphosis. The daily reality of blank walls with little or no visual stimulation forced him to find some method of expression. While in isolation, Nora conceived the mental blueprint of his most precious dream, a pink house unique among those in Northport. This house and its creation consumed him. Nora used his dream to get through some extraordinarily challenging times.

Living in a makeshift post–World War II mental treatment program was no picnic. As I'm sure you can imagine, it was a harrowing experience for Nora, though fortunately he wasn't one of the "Tuskeegee Six." A nurse named Miss Naggers befriended Nora and in times of desperation would console him. She told him, "You can make it if you try," and that he did. With his dreams, the unfailing support of Annie Bell, and methods of meditation, Nora fought his way back from the brink of insanity. When Annie returned home, he was released to her on a three-month-in, three-month-out basis.

Nora was hailed as the hero returned home. Annie Bell took care of him while he reintroduced himself to family and friends. Nora's concern was not with them, though. He took an immediate interest in us, the children. He was especially interested in me. I must have looked pretty bad at that point, a fat little handicapped boy in casts, but Nora asked me what was going on. When I told him I was attempting to walk he did not laugh at me, merely encouraged me to try.

During Uncle Nora's times at home those first two years, we became very close. He wanted to teach me all he could so I would become more self-confident and independent. He and Sam taught me to tell time by practicing with me until I could count from one to one hundred, and then placing a clock on the television, while PBS broadcast a program for children on how to tell time. Whenever the time was announced, I was made to look at the clock until I connected the time announced with the position of the clock hands. We spent many afternoons watching PBS programs, which proved vital to my early education.

As Uncle shared the hardships he encountered during his stay at the VA hospital, I could relate to his isolation. Nora, like myself, understood how it felt to be a prisoner of circumstances beyond control. As he recounted his experiences in the war, I realized the extent of his patriotism. Nora also believed in the importance of pride in our heritage and impoverished background. My uncle always used to say, "If you forget where you come from, you may end up there again."

In 1964, my life took many paradoxical twists and turns. At the same time that my despair began to increase, over my inability to walk, so did the occurrence of many new opportunities in my life. One day that summer, a social worker from the county welfare office came driving up to the house with some exciting news about a new program in special education. The Northington School, situated where University Mall is now, had been selected to be part of an experimental attempt at integrated learning between handicapped children and their able-bodied peers.

Aunt Annie Bell sat on the porch with me and pondered the information, then turned toward the house and yelled inside. "Hey Ada, why ain't Nathan in school wit' de other children?"

"He cain't learn nuthin'."

"Oh yeah? Well he is goin' to be in school wit' them dat ain't learnin' nuthin'!"

Auntie refused to accept Momma's notion that I was not capable of learning. Others in the family knew, as Auntie was beginning to discover, that I was not ignorant at all. In fact, there were signs that I was actually quite intelligent. For example, whenever anyone needed to remember some event occurring in the future, they would rely on me. I have, to this day, the ability to recall information almost verbatim.

In April, Annie Bell scheduled a doctor's appointment for July thirteenth, and she told me about it. When the day came, I reminded her when she first woke up, "A . . . A . . . Auntie, remember yo' d . . . doctor's appointment." Things like that tipped Auntie off to the fact that there was a brain in my head, a brain she felt deserved a chance for the educational opportunity that social worker had spoken of.

I already had a positive attitude about education from hearing the neighborhood children talk with one another while at play and on their way to school. I envied the other kids and wanted a chance to go, too. Being inquisitive and highly motivated, I could never understand why I had to stay at home when I instinctively had an aptitude for learning. I'm thankful that Auntie and Uncle felt the same, regardless of Momma's repeated attempts to shield and protect me from the outside world. I felt that perhaps by attending school, I would eventually share something in common with other children my own age.

I knew by this time I would never walk, and prescription drugs were becoming my crutch. Once the doctors and therapists at Crippled Children's Services accepted my lameness, they suggested that I be fitted into a child-sized wheelchair. This was a good idea (although it was embarrassing at the time), because I was too heavy to be carried and needed a way to be mobile while attending classes.

When I officially began my public school education in the late summer of 1964, thanks to the new Civil Rights Bill requiring integration of schools, a new world opened up to me. I entered the first grade at ten years of age, and I will never forget the expression on my teacher's face when I was wheeled into her classroom for the first time. Her reactions, as typical today as in the 1960s, were filled with anxiety, frustration, and confusion.

Teachers at that time were not given any formal training or preparation enabling them to address the needs of their disabled students. Because people with disabilities were typically kept at home or placed in nursing homes or institutions, they were almost never enrolled in public school. As education in a public school setting became a growing trend for disabled students, many teachers were left at a great disadvantage. They were almost as frightened and vulnerable as we were, and the academy had to adapt, develop, and incorporate programs at the college level to better equip elementary and secondary school teachers in their efforts.

The students were even more unprepared than the faculty. We entered the room, and all class activity stopped suddenly. Everyone turned toward us and kept staring, as a silence of unfamiliarity and trepidation momentarily filled the room. We were placed off to the side of the classroom and down in the front, fully in view of some thirty or so children sitting at their desks. That whole first experience was really unsettling. It made me feel like some kind of zoo animal or circus attraction, rather than a student.

The situation got progressively worse. The faculty at Northington decided that keeping disabled students in each classroom did more harm than good. They felt that, since the students had enough problems dealing with racial conflicts, keeping us in class was an unnecessary added distraction. We were separated into adjacent rooms, isolated from the regular students.

Each handicapped "pod," as they were called, had a teacher assigned to instruct us in rudimentary education to fit our own working pace. Every day we were drilled in fundamentals. I watched with curiosity as big words were thrown around that everyone understood but me. I nodded and smiled but basically remained clueless.

Miss McDowell was like a drill sergeant. She had a very grim looking face that could peel the paint off a wall. Most everyone but me was working at the same pace. It took me a while to grasp complicated concepts. Miss McDowell and Miss South, our other teacher, grew frustrated with me because I wasn't as sophisticated as the other students. The only other handicapped student in the pod with me who was black was Doris McGee, who had been given home tutoring and came from a more economically advantaged background than I.

I believe economic advantage adds many beneficial, subtle intangibles to family life. Economic advantage increases the chances for children to learn classroom etiquette and social graces in the home. Also, generally speaking, the value of education will likewise be handed down from parents or other family authority figures to children. Statistically speaking, the opportunity for both parents to hold college diplomas in said households is greater.

Momma, though unschooled, valued education for every child she had but me. While we were children, though she herself was unable to read, Momma tried to provide an environment that was conducive to learning. Sheila, Ray, and Christine received diplomas from Stillman College, Cheyney State in Pennsylvania, and the University of Alabama in Tuscaloosa, respectively. All of them have utilized their education to raise their own standard of living.

Doris McGee was originally from Mississippi. Her father was a minister, and her mother worked in some kind of factory. She acquired her disability when her father accidentally backed over her legs in the driveway. She was just four years old and was forever paralyzed from the waist down. The accident brought the family close together and placed Doris in a position to grow into an extraordinary person.

When a disabled child is born and the circumstances are ambiguous, the unresolved guilt at the possibility of parental fault decays the heart of otherwise noble and stable parents. I have seen this in my own home and in the homes of friends. Parents of children born disabled may need to realize that this is not their fault. It is not the fault of anyone, only a physical, spiritual, and mental challenge. Burden or not, it is important for parents to understand that in all forty-five of my years I have never met a disabled child that didn't take pleasure in the simplest aspects of daily living.

Situations like Doris McGee's and mine, where our mental states are adequate enough to take on a forgiving attitude, make the family strong. After all, God made us this way, and only He has ultimate control over how a child is born. Look for the lessons in experiences with your child, and consider yourself blessed to witness the power of God. Wisdom comes in helping a disabled child develop into a productive human being, "productive" being a matter of perspective. Allow your child to teach you his/her value and what is important in this life.

In my pod were two other students besides me and Doris: Snow Cannon and Frank Goins. Our chronological ages ranged from ten to fourteen years, Frank was the oldest and I was youngest. I remember my first encounter with Snow Cannon. He tried his best to communicate by spelling each word on his alphabet board. Although I was unable to read, Snow was imaginative and could bypass my deficiency by communicating through appropriate gestures and facial expressions. I found that we shared several common interests.

Frank Goins was from the country. He walked on crutches because of spastic diplegia, one form of cerebral palsy. Everyone liked Frank. He excelled in English and had a pleasant personality that could lighten the mood during touchy moments in the classroom.

"Nathan, can you tell me how to spell 'rat'?"

"Uh . . . Uh . . . Yeah, Miss McDowell, I can spell 'rat.' Is it . . . uh . . . R-E-T?"

(Hysterical laughter from the gallery, as Miss McDowell approaches my desk in severe consternation.)

"R-E-T?!?"

Slamming her hand down on the desk, she grits her teeth, hissing, "Try it again."

"Uh . . . Uh . . . R-I-T??"

She grew more and more impatient with me as time went on. I'm a slow learner, but once I do learn something I never forget it. Miss McDowell became guilty of a common dilemma for teachers who educate children with exceptionality. Between my skin color and my disability, she brushed me aside after a few attempts. Ah, what a difference between appearance and reality!

Many people challenge the value in educating severely disabled students up to a high school diploma. I am living, breathing proof that those opponents are mistaken. How many children disfigured by one physical disability or another are labeled as mentally inept? How many disabled children remain neglected and undervalued?

My disabled friends, black and white, made the affront of daily prejudice easier to deal with, but you never really get used to it. We were not allowed to move about in the halls until faculty and students had moved on to other activities. It was believed that this tactic would avoid confrontation and unexpected misbehavior or interaction with us. We used the playground alone and had our own entrance to a storage area behind the lunchroom where reluctant school faculty fed us while the other kids ate in the main dining hall. A rickety and dangerous catwalk connected the buildings. We were wheeled across it and exposed to the outside elements while everyone else was allowed to move about inside the building.

In an effort to relieve mounting tension, resentment, and unrest, some teachers conducted mini-tours to let other students view the "handicapped" kids. As the children approached cautiously and gathered at the door, they began to stare. The teachers explained that "they can not walk as we can." Some children cried, some laughed and were consequently scolded, but what got to me was the way most of them gaped at us. Again, I felt like some roadside attraction or sideshow freak.

The mini-tours were not helpful; in fact, they were hellish. Instead of encouraging friendship and understanding, they called undue attention to our respective disabilities. By the end of my first year of school, I hated my education, my wheelchair, even life itself. The drugs I had been taking for pain only served to weaken my constitution and foul up my attitude. Nora was permanently released toward the end of that same year, and not a moment too soon.

Dry Rot Syndrome

As I mentioned previously, "Dry Rot Syndrome" began with a combination of negativity in both my personal feelings and daily experiences. I was almost simultaneously bombarded with racism, legal drug addiction, peer pressure, puberty, and the stress of a quasi-elementary school education. In addition, there were other things going on, things which are difficult for me to talk about even today.

Abuse is not an easy subject to address, especially when it involves family, but I feel it is necessary to bring this to light for the benefit of everyone with physical disabilities, the infirm, and all other victims of physical, sexual, or emotional abuse. Piled on top of my ever-greater comprehension of the difference between the handicapped versus those who are not, my abuse created the deepening hole of depression and despair which I fell into head first.

Momma had a close friend, whom we will refer to as Gladys. She lived two doors down from us. Gladys was a middle-aged attractive lady, about thirty-five or forty. She was decidedly aggressive in her pursuit of men and was very sick. One day, Momma left me at home while she went to the store to buy groceries. Everyone else was away at school, and Sam was working. I was sitting on the couch watching television when Gladys knocked on the door.

"Nathan, where is yo' mom?"

"Momma is gone to de store. She'll be back after 'while."

"Nathan, what are you watchin' on TV? Can I watch wit' chu?"

"Yeah . . . Yeah."

"You sure is a fine boy. I'm gone show you sump's, an don't chou tell nobody, because if you do, sump' bad is gone happen to you."

"What chou mean sump' bad gone happen to me?"

"You do like I tell you, an' won't nuthin' happen to you. And don't you tell nobody! Hear me, Nathan?"

"Yeah . . . Yeah."

For the next couple of minutes, I became the object of this woman's sexual domination. She pulled up her dress, took her panties off, and pulled her body closer, telling me not to move. She then proceeded to get my penis and insert it into her vagina. Gladys raped me and put the fear of God in me to keep me silent. She stayed long enough to tell me, if I opened my mouth to anyone, something disastrous would happen. When Momma returned, she immediately knew something was wrong, but could find out nothing. I was crying uncontrollably.

Years later, I told Nora about that day. He said, "Son, this ain't your fault. I feel your pain, Nate. This kind of thing happens all the time, and you have hid this long enough. You need to tell your Momma about this, but I will respect your wishes and keep it between you and me." Uncle went on to share with me his theory that my feelings of inadequacy were largely a result of this incident.

It took me fourteen years to confront my feelings concerning this. I have no resentment in my heart for her now, only pity. You see, sexual abuse is a common plight affecting many people, but it is especially prevalent in the disabled community. Every time I think about my experience and then see the newest scandal on television, it incenses me that it is still happening in institutions and homes today, when the ability to promote awareness has increased so much.

Maybe eliminating abuse is, like ending other undesirable aspects of human nature, impossible. Some theories blame class, others race, and still others dysfunctional families. I know that anger is our nature, regardless of the cause. I try to offer my life in service to God, and I pray. Prayer will go a long way toward healing yourself, believe me. I never cease to be amazed at the variety of ways prayer gets answered in my life, often in forms I don't recognize at first.

Racial controversies were foreign to me before I started school. Governor George C. Wallace stood blocking the entrance of Vivian Malone and James Hood to Foster Auditorium on the University of Alabama campus only a year before I started elementary school. I felt the heated anguish of racial injustice for the first time at Northington.

Even then, I did not realize that the horrible pain I felt being called "colored" and "nigger" by the white children at school could extend into the outside world, until I heard a black disabled classmate named Peter Moore tell unsettling stories about the black limousine that followed his mother every day as she drove him to and from school. Peter expressed his mother's terror and imitated her facial expression when she glanced into the rearview mirror. His mother was convinced it was the Ku Klux Klan and feared for the safety of Peter and herself! As it turns out, the car was really an FBI escort assigned to protect them from groups like the Klan or anyone else who tried to block Peter from getting his education.

I remember those awful Northington softball games we played during my first year. They were a futile attempt to involve us in play with the other children. Peter, Frank, Snow, and I posed as bases for the other children to run around. As we were teased by able-bodied kids, I felt more like a pile of manure than part of the game. At home, neighborhood children used to laugh at my wheelchair and throw rocks into the spokes. I loved being raced around by my brothers because I knew they would never hurt me, but others had fun at my expense, and I used to fall whenever I tried to defend myself.

One day I was sitting in the yard, when a neighborhood kid named Oscar Ivory came right up and scratched me hard across my face. I began to cry hysterically, as blood poured out of the open wound. A few days later, when he had forgotten the incident, Oscar came within reach of my good arm. I had forgotten nothing and grabbed the back of his shirt collar. I beat his head up against the porch until Aunt Joyce heard the screaming and came out to free him from my death grip. Funny thing is, we are now good friends.

The kids used to run around me yelling their nickname for the funny looking and sounding kid in the wheelchair. They used to call me "Helicopter Arms," because of my spastic right arm and the limited range of motion I have in my left. The physical bruises I suffered were nothing compared to the emotional damage those supposed games did to my already fragile self-esteem.

I began puberty at eleven years of age, pretty early for a male. Besides the difficulty of sometimes intense growing pains, I was experiencing new feelings, unfamiliar to me before. I looked at girls in a different way and liked what I saw. My older brother had many girlfriends in high school, and they were the most beautiful girls I had ever seen. Sometimes, late at night, he would tell me about kissing them and what it was like to be close to them. Needless to say, this was exciting stuff for me. I used to imagine what it must be like, and although Milton said my time would come, I had my doubts. Why would any girl want me?

I channeled all of this negativity into my drug usage, the schedule that had become the center of my life. Aunt Annie Bell saw what was going on and tried to cheer me up, but I grew more violent and unpredictable as the days passed.

"Nathan, we is goin' to look at de Christmas lights. Do you want to come?"

"No! The hell w . . . wit' you and yo' d . . . damn lights!"

"Chile, you better watch yo' mouth!"

"Go on! Leave! G . . . Git outta here! L . . . Leave me the hell alone!"

And she would exit in a huff, feeling helpless and hurt. This trend continued for quite a while. When she or Momma complained to the doctors, they only increased my dosage. On Easter Saturday, 1965, right before Nora's release, I went really out of control. The adults went fishing that afternoon, and I wanted to come along. As usual, I was in trouble for cussing and misbehavior earlier that week, and Auntie refused to allow me to participate. My brothers were also left behind. Because I couldn't go, they couldn't go either. "Someone must stay at home and tend to Nathan," Auntie instructed. They were not happy with me.

As soon as Auntie and Momma were gone, I went on an indignant rampage, destroying furniture, marking up the front door, breaking lamps and anything else I could get my hand on before I collapsed from exhaustion. My brothers, Milton and Ray, were only too happy to oblige, knowing I would be blamed because of the wheelchair marks all over the place. When Auntie returned, she was highly upset, to say the least. I had the worst beating of my life that day, and I caused no more trouble at home. Instead, I turned my anger gut-bound, inward.

Uncle Nora came to my rescue with characteristic patience and understanding, which he continually shared from the first day he entered my life. Once he was released for good, our occasional talks together became a daily routine. He found me at first to be virtually unresponsive, and it scared him. Nora stayed with me most of the time that first summer, trying to divert my attention by playing cards, dominoes, and checkers, solving jigsaw puzzles, and through discourse. I was unable to concentrate for more than a few minutes at a time. Thankfully, we were able to communicate despite my critical situation. Uncle never gave up on me.

Auntie and Uncle Nora wasted little time making Nora's dream-house fantasy into reality. He arranged for the purchase of some land across from us, which had previously been our neighborhood playing field. As the land was excavated and prepared for laying the foundation, we would sit together under the cherry tree and talk. Uncle was a shy and private person. After nineteen years of being cloistered from the world, he was not much better than I at confiding in people. As we grew closer, he shared a part of himself with me that no one else has ever seen. Our talks helped him as much as they helped me.

Initially, we talked mostly about his dream house. I learned the importance of following my own special star. Using the design and long-awaited creation of his house as an example, Uncle reminded me that no one has the power to destroy our dreams unless we allow them to. As he described each stage of development the house would undergo, the glow in his face was priceless and inspiring.

As Uncle Nora recalled his painful experiences, I could make a direct correlation with my own. While fruitlessly attempting to walk, I suffered various types of treatment for six years. At the same time, and for many years before my birth, Uncle was suffering isolation and loneliness to a degree of mental anguish I can only imagine. He taught me that various forms of imprisonment exist. This helped me learn to accept my wheelchair, not as a form of bondage, but as an extension of freedom.

He taught me to expand my mind by always approaching things from a different perspective. He maintained that nothing in life is limited to one point of view and to always explore the alternatives. Allow me to offer an example of one method he used to prove this point. It requires you to follow some simple rules.

Obtain a school notebook or piece of loose-leaf paper. If applicable, tear out a blank page as close to the edge as possible, then discard the notebook and hold the piece of paper at arm's length for as long as it takes to observe as much as you can about it. I'm looking for five things in particular. When you think you have them all, pick this book back up and continue reading.

If you noticed everything, then you have done well. As I describe each characteristic of the piece of paper, put yourself in the shoes of young Nathan, as I explain things to you the way my uncle did for me.

First, the shape is rectangular. Hold up the paper in the way of its most narrow block of your line of vision, and it remains at least partially visible. The rectangle can be viewed from different angles, as can many problems within your life. Second, notice the thickness of the paper. The page is quite thin. If you ball up the paper, it becomes thicker. Its thickness represents the severity of your dilemma. Similarly, a situation can appear more complicated than it is in reality. Take the time to sort things out before making an overly hasty judgment.

Third, there are several blue lines running parallel all up and down the page. Each line symbolizes a different solution to any obstacle. Each one is unique and there are many, symbolic of the variety of answers that exist for you to examine.

Fourth, the red line intersecting every blue line is the road you will take on your journey toward a new outlook on life. It includes every available solution to your problem.

Finally, if you examine the page closely, you will notice that it is not really one solid color but a variety of hues. Nothing is really black or white, only gray. The experiences we all encounter and cultures that enrich our individual personal experience are incorporated within our own mosaic, hence the entire page before you. My reason for sharing this with you is to make it clear: Make something out of your life, instead of letting it make something of you.

If you remain paralized by indecision, don't be surprised if at some point you peer into the mirror, see your reflection, and dislike what you find. Everyone has a crutch of one sort or another if they don't know God. God has a hand ready to reach out for anyone who is in despair over attempts to ease their soul with the fruits of this life. He is searching for you before you are seeking Him. I have reason to believe, based on my experience, that all those who accept that they need Him first and then reach out in prayer will be answered without exception.

Uncle helped me to see how important it is to examine all options before making a life-changing decision. I'm not saying I was on an easy road in light of how befuddled my mind was by various substances and denials. I would never have been strong enough to take on my hardest challenge alone, and it was on the horizon.

Cold Turkey

My reflexes were becoming increasingly sluggish, and I was unable to organize or clarify my thoughts. School, home, inside, awake or asleep, I was indifferent to the world around me. I have never encountered such a wild array of psychedelic phenomena as I did during those last three months before my salvation and awakening. The walls around my strange inner sanctum went out of focus, developing into a serpentine pattern. The light around me would shift and change as it became sinuous hues of red, blue, pink, violet, orange, and green. My urine even had a funny color and a pungent odor.

After three years of dependency, I had become reclusive, introverted, sullen, distractible, undisciplined, and withdrawn. Uncle Nora was terribly worried about me. He determined the time had come to eliminate the drugs before they deteriorated my brain and body any further. He and Auntie took matters into their own hands, by removing my medication cold turkey. I protested like crazy, screaming and crying to no avail. My body coiled into agonizing spasms, as I broke into a chilly sweat, flailing my arms about, during the first six to eight hours of withdrawal.

These initial symptoms were devastating, as I fell prey to a powerful ache firmly rooted in my mind and body. My fantasy world splintered as my body exploded into ferocious tremors. My head felt like a bouncing ball on the end of a string. A thousand fingers pulled apart my brain, stretching it like taffy. Snakes crawled all over me and monsters chased me as I burst forth from the shell which had become my home.

As my body's craving increased, survival became a minute-to-minute crisis situation. My body erupted in flames, and I couldn't control the trembling or tears. In desperation, I cried aloud for even one little pill. I tried bribing my brothers and sisters, even begging Auntie and Uncle like a dog. Their conviction was iron. Even Momma could not be broken down.

Uncle never left my side. As he steadfastly refused to give in, Nora kept telling me that he was doing this out of love, and love alone. Because the depth of his compassion was great, Uncle was able to internalize my precarious state of mind and my inability to win the fight alone. Taking me gently into his big arms, Uncle Nora squeezed me tightly.

"Nate, I done tol' you dat what I'm doin' is gonna help you in de long run."

"I . . . I . . . I need a pill right now Uncle Nora. It hurts . . . it hurts so bad."

"You ain't gettin' no more damn medicine boy, not now, not ever!"

"But if I don't get no mo' medicine, I'll die."

"Then you can die, dammit, cause you ain't gettin' none."

Eventually my body collapsed and my eyes closed. I felt as though a lumberjack was sawing my brain, ripping back and forth, until I drifted off into a deep and feverish sleep.

Uncle's experiences enabled him to travel effortlessly into my world, and together we fought our way back to sobriety. As I began to see the wisdom of what he was trying to communicate, my agony became more bearable. We practiced methods of meditation that calmed my struggling body and helped me regain a grip on the world. Nora's advice and solace prepared me to face life with greater courage and conviction.

Recognizing the value in a drug-free life at twelve or thirteen years old, after being on drugs for eight years, wasn't something I did alone. I used to sit for hours enjoying the radio. I was listening, after a discussion with Uncle Nora, when I first heard Gil Scott-Heron singing. "The Bottle" and "Angel Dust" were two of the first songs I ever heard about alcoholism or the abuse of other substances. Gil's music has helped me through many tribulations and has often described unclear thoughts of my own in words I couldn't have expressed better.

The next appointment at Crippled Children's Services became a fiery debate. The doctors explained to Auntie, Nora, and Momma that it was necessary to continue my "treatment." The family would have no part of it.

"Why is Nathan off the drugs we have prescribed?"

"Nora and I decided that it was time for Nathan to stop takin' these damn drugs."

"Who decided that Nathan should be taken off without our authorization?"

"It were a joint decision by his mother, me, an' Annie Bell."

"All he do is sleep. De poor boy don't even know he in the world."

"He weigh a lot more than when he was first put on dem drugs, an' he ain't his self no mo'."

"We understand your concerns about the effects of these drugs, but let me assure you, we know what we are doing."

"Oh no hell you don't know what you doin'! This boy gonna die if he keep bein' on these drugs, an' he ain't gonna be on these damn drugs no more! Do you understand me?"

The doctors assured Auntie they would make certain I was placed back on drug therapy as soon as possible. Nora rebutted the doctors politely, but firmly. My family would not watch me suffer and waste away any further. That was the end of it. The doctors realized my family was adamant about their decision and no amount of discussion would change their minds.

Once we returned home, Uncle and I continued to fight the gripping stranglehold of drug dependency together. It's a misunderstood disease, chemical addiction, because you don't ever stop fighting it, really. It's not like anyone can say, "Okay, I beat it, no more cigarettes/alcohol/cocaine/heroin/crack." Anyone addicted to something must face it on a minute-to-minute basis. So many factors are not seen by those on the outside who are often more comfortable with criticism than in offering aid, assistance, or solace.

Had I voluntarily experimented with drugs or not, it wouldn't have mattered to Uncle Nora. He was more concerned about how to aid his nephew in finding more value living without drugs, than with how it started or whose fault it was. He respected my need for privacy and was never critical or judgmental, offering constructive advice and welcome comfort whenever I asked. He helped me develop a mental sheet of armor against the desire for substance use, showing me my self-worth and giving me faith.

I applied Uncle's teachings to life at Northington once I was able to continue my studies that fall. The struggle toward black dignity had escalated by 1966. Attending school in the heat of racial strife made my disability appear secondary by comparison. Though at the age of twelve, racial conflict was beyond my ability to comprehend, overcoming the negative stereotype of being labeled "handicapped" was not. Instead of humiliating me, my wheelchair would soon remind me that I was unusually significant and unique.

My education had again reached the pinnacle of my priorities. No one at Northington seemed that interested in helping me to do much. It seems as though their attitude was something like "you're lucky you're here at all," so it was, as always, up to me to make as much as I could out of the little I had. I'll tell you straight up that in six years I never saw one teacher make an honest effort to educate disabled or black students. My predicament remained unchanged, and I didn't learn to read, but I did meet an interesting character that fall I've referenced before, by the name of Peter Moore.

Peter

"Here come the human doormat, y'all, wit' his old, green, torn-up wheelchair!"

"I ain't got no t . . . torn up wheelchair no more, Peter Moore. My chair is brand new a . . . a . . . an' as good as yours."

"That scrap-metal junkyard with the new puke green cushion may be as good as my spare chair, but chou ain't."

"W . . . What chou mean by d . . . dat?"

"What I mean by that is you can't feed yo'self, you can't talk, and your helicopter arms fly around all the time like you are fixin' to take off or something. Why don't you talk like you got a brain in your fat head, fat boy?"

I couldn't respond. This pudgy kid with the devilishly arrogant grin made life at Northington hell for me from day one of fall 1968. I grew more furious as I thought about his daily taunts, because he was right and I knew it. Most people couldn't understand a word I spoke. It took great effort to put my thoughts into words of any kind because of my speech impediment.

The family always fed me. Momma refused to let me feed myself unless I insisted. Then she would get offended, like I'm too good to be tended to by her. Peter made me think for the first time about shame and dignity. Why couldn't I feed myself? Why couldn't I talk? Why couldn't I control my arms? Peter brought this out, in no uncertain terms, as brutally honest as possible.

As we engaged in mental gymnastics, Peter's darting barbs and sarcasm evolved into carefully orchestrated contests of personal endurance and awareness. As my resistance increased, Peter was more determined than ever to show me my own inadequacies in contrast to his polish. Daily bouts of one-upmanship set in motion intense change within, as I began to take up for myself.

James David Moore, alias Peter Moore, was a master of the English language, a rare case among black disabled youth even today, and he loved cornering me into a duel of wits. When we discussed our disabilities and other problems that accompanied them, he never let me evade the reality of my own unstable attitude and misgivings. Peter badgered me about my inability to assert myself when others called me names. He poked and prodded at me incessantly, but never ridiculed something that was beyond my ability to change.

I didn't like Peter at first. We spent more than three years in peer warfare, his pointing out to everyone my lack of sophistication, as I gradually developed the tools to fight back. Thanks to him, my English improved dramatically, as I began to hear it spoken properly around Northington, especially and usually painfully out of Peter's smart-assed mouth. If no one would teach me to read, I would begin learning to speak, by God. True enough, I couldn't beat Peter in the classroom by a long shot, but there were other methods of revenge.

Each of our little contests was a fight to the death. I distinctly remember one wheelchair race that held significance for both of us. Peter was despondent that day, and I couldn't understand why. When he refused to share his feelings, I challenged him to a race, and he accepted, despite his somber mood. After all, with my flailing arms and pathetic coordination, I had never beaten him before. He felt invincible.

When recess came, Frank, as usual, lined us up alongside one another in the hallway so that neither Peter nor I held an advantageous position. Doris, halfway between the start and finish line, cried out, "Get ready . . . Set . . . GO!"

We were off down the hall! Peter propelled himself forward at a speed quicker than usual. He laughed out loud, calling me a "caboose," as he took an early lead. I entered the race with dogged determination and a quiet smile, grabbing onto doorknobs and armrails to pull myself along. As he approached the finish line, to his shock and surprise, I whipped out in front of him and won the race by a large margin.

Peter didn't know I had been planning this little game for quite some time. All week, I saved my milk money and drank water at lunch. After school on Thursday I sent my friends around to the corner store for cookies and candy, while I waited on the front porch. Friday morning before Peter had arrived, I'd secretly bribed Doris and Frank into helping me in the race. They had previously positioned themselves for my benefit.

Frank's push from behind kept me going in a straight line. Doris stayed over to my left, in case I needed her for backup. I grabbed onto her wheelchair for that extra boost that helped me win. Peter, with all of his foolish pride, was unaware of any covert activity. When he found out what happened, he was really mad. That race marked the first time I had ever outsmarted him. "That's why you were drinking water all week, you fool!" was all he could manage, as I laughed hysterically.

A week or so later, Peter informed me that we were going to have a spelling test. The test, he said, would cover only three of the five lessons we had gone over in class. I thanked him for reminding me about the test and studied the chapters he had spoken of with Uncle Nora that night. The next morning, Peter burst out laughing at the expression on my face when I was given a test covering all five chapters! Bad grades were my greatest fear, and he had settled the score.

Peter loved tonguetwisters, like "Peter picked a peck of pickled peppers," and "She sells sea shells down by the sea shore." He knew with my marked speech impediment, I would never be able to articulate these with any degree of clarity or skill. Although vocal eloquence helped him maintain a definite edge over me, the practice of such riddles greatly improved my ability to speak clearly. By the spring of 1969, with the help of Milton and my baby sister, Sheila, I had the bare rudiments of reading under my belt. I could read on a first-grade level.

Peter had progressive muscular dystrophy (MD), making him wheelchair-bound at age ten. His disability gradually transformed his muscle tissue into fatty (lipid) tissue, incapacitating him more with each passing year. In spite of his worsening condition, Peter was determined to keep a positive attitude. Self-pity was never part of his vocabulary. We began to value each other's strengths and weaknesses, as Peter began to realize over time that I could help him also.

My friends and I studied hard at Northington. As graduation approached, I was very downcast. Peter was headed for middle school, but I was left behind. It nearly broke my heart when the school board decided that I was "implacable" within the system; it seemed like an excuse. I was sixteen years old, and wanted an active and direct course of action for charting my future. I felt robbed of my key by the very same people who opened the door to begin with!

Uncle and I discussed the situation at great length. He assured me that learning could occur in any setting and promised to be my teacher following graduation. I was too miserable to listen at first, but Uncle was determined to get through my stubborn adolescent skull. At that age I knew everything. School was finished, life was over, and that was it. Period. Nora would smile and muse to himself as I ranted and raved at him about my "final days of education."

Graduation ceremonies were held in May of 1970. I sadly said farewell to my Northington classmates. I would miss them all, but the possibility of never seeing Peter again was more than I could bear. As Auntie and Uncle put me in the car for the ride home, I broke down and cried.

"Boy, what chou cryin' 'bout now?"

"It ain't fair Unc . . . Uncle Nora. Why cain't I keep on goin'?"

"Nate, you gonna find out there is nuthin' in life dat is fair, and all things whether dey good or bad, will end. I done tol' you already, you don't need no classroom to get chou an education."

"Dammit! I hate dis here place anyway! I ain't never gonna learn nuthin' again, and I ain't gonna see my friends no mo'."

"Boy, I'm gonna kick your ass in gear now. Dere ain't no room in dis here car for yo' bad attitude."

Occasionally, Nora got firm with me. He listened avidly, but when it reached a saturation point, Uncle told me that he could not live my life or solve all my problems. His attempts to motivate me toward a climate of self-reliance paid off. After a week of feeling sorry for myself, I acquiesced, calling him into the room for a chat. I turned toward the window, grinning sheepishly as he quietly opened the door.

"Unc . . . Uncle Nora? I'm just bein' stubborn."

"Son, you give me a chance now. I ain't been wrong yet. You gotta think bigger, my boy."

"You right. True enough, so listen. I'm ready, willin', and able. I ain't goin' nowhere. Like, let's do it. Let's go!"

Can an Education Help Me?

Uncle Nora taught me much, but his lessons were geared less toward "the three Rs" and more toward improving my self-image through awakening me to the glory of learning new skills and information. The first thing he required me to do was pick up a "Dick and Jane" book so I could begin reading the pages he had selected. Any book was extremely difficult for me to grasp. When I asked for help, Nora refused, saying I must figure out a way to pick it up myself or I was never going to learn anything. It took me ten or fifteen minutes before I could knock the book close enough to grab the narrow binding with my left hand and place it on my lap. Every time I tried to open it the book would fall, and I would start again.

After repeated scenarios, I devised a way of securing the book's hardbound cover under my leg straps. Although they helped hold it some of the time, my flailing right arm kept getting in the way, knocking the book onto the floor. Once able to lift open the outer cover, I had great difficulty turning the pages. They were too slick to grasp with only two fingers and a thumb. Seeing my honest determination, Uncle Nora helped me when absolutely necessary, though this became less needed with time.

Toward the end of August, 1970, a letter arrived at the house addressed to me. I was so excited! I had never received mail before and nearly burst with curiosity over what it said.

"Momma, dis letter here got Nathan's name on it."

"Open . . . Open . . . Open dis letter here! Open it Sam! I got to find out what it say!"

"Shut yo' mouth boy, I'm openin' it as fast as I can!"

"What it say? What do . . . does it say?"

"It says dat some program want chou to come an' be part of it, Nathan. Now, I don't know about dat."

"But it'd be a way fo' me to go on wit' my education, Momma!"

"Jus' a waste of time. What good an education gonna do you in your condition? You got to realize, Nathan, that chou's a handicap, an' we don' have the time to take you to these programs. It's enough jus' to git chou up in the mornin' an' I got to go to work."

It took the entire three weeks before the initial party at the Hackberry Summer Program just to convince Momma I should attend. Although she originally refused, I had begun, thanks to my experiences at Northington and Uncle Nora's gentle persuasion, to question and form opinions related to decisions that were made for me, instead of by me. When I learned at the party that Peter, Frank, Doris, and Snow were already there learning, I was thrilled and determined to get involved!

To this day I don't know why Momma was so highly against my getting an education. By this time, she already had one daughter in college, my sister Christine. She encouraged every one of my brothers and sisters to go to school, except me. I guess she was just being overprotective of me. I love her very much, and she knows the value of my pursuits today.

After graduation from Northington, I remained at home with Nora. He helped me continue to improve my reading and social skills. The Hackberry Summer Day Camp, held at the University of Alabama during the summer of 1973, was one of a few innovative programs for the disabled in the state back then. In 1972, Dr. Loretta Holder, the founder of the program, had helped convince Momma that I could benefit from what it had to offer. Nonetheless, it took a full year before all the arrangements could be made allowing me to participate.

Excepting the party in August 1970, I had not seen or heard from my friends at Northington since graduation, and being reunited with them was great. Peter and I were dramatically different, but we complemented each other. Despite MD, he had become more lyrical, linguistic, and musical. Peter shared poems, short stories, and musical compositions with me that were more beautiful than anything I'd ever heard before. I had developed into a more analytical and reflective person, with Uncle Nora's help, but was primarily the same risk-taker and outspoken fellow he had helped me become.

He admired my tenacity and vivaciousness. I marveled yet at his almost effortless ability to communicate with others. Once again we found a way to compete, as in the old days. Peter wanted to match wits with me over board games, a new hobby of his, specifically the game of chess.

The idea of playing fascinated me. He was an ace chess player, and I wanted to challenge him in an area requiring a high level of skill. We began to play the game religiously. My fine-motor skills improved dramatically as we played daily at camp and nightly over the phone. He was merciless and brilliant, never giving me an inch until I earned it. Once I developed a certain degree of prowess, he would change his technique, completely confusing me again. Years later, I defeated him in a major chess tournament.

Camping began at eight o'clock each morning and ran until four o'clock in the afternoon. Dr. Holder arranged for a university van to pick up and drop off students who, like myself, had no available means of transportation. The Hackberry Summer Program provided a haven for about ten young adults with a wide variety of disabilities. Their conditions included, but were not limited to, mental retardation, autism, cerebral palsy, and muscular dystrophy. The program was staffed with graduate-level teachers, interns, practicum students, and volunteers.

Hackberry not only opened doors for us, it paved the way for a revolutionary new program in the state of Alabama, the Adult Work Activity Center. This evolved into what is currently known as West Alabama Comprehensive Services, where research was conducted for the creation of the Rule Infant Simulation Environment (RISE) program. We founded the center on Tuesday, September 18, 1973.

Striving for Independence

Dr. Loretta Holder began her tenure at the University of Alabama in 1972. She arrived at a time when educating students with disabilities was on the forefront of the country's political agenda. Dr. Holder recognized the plight of disabled students within the system. With courage and professional commitment, she took on the challenge of orchestrating change. She and Dr. Bill Heller organized and proposed a unique and experimental day-training program for physically disabled young adults.

Dr. Holder encountered tremendous obstacles during her struggle to secure state funding for this special program. Skeptical colleagues suspected she was wasting her time. Programming for post–school-age disabled young adults was not a high priority, when it seemed easier and less expensive to warehouse them within the home or other institutions. The Hackberry Summer Program received funding but was only the beginning of her vision. Dr. Holder was steadfast in her belief that offering the disabled every opportunity to develop their skills and talents ensures their ability to make meaningful contributions to public life.

The Department of Mental Health of the state of Alabama reviewed and evaluated their proposal. The project received federal funding, and the Adult Work Activity Center became the envisioned reality. Peter, Snow, Frank, and I were the first students at the center, then a model demonstration project. For us, this was a revolutionary educational opportunity. It was awe-inspiring to be part of an environment specifically planned and designed to meet our needs.

I learned very quickly that this was going to be a completely new experience. Jane Shaw, our first teacher, and Bettye Roberts, her assistant, struggled with me that first year at the center. They had difficulty penetrating my stubbornness and verbal obscenities. Communicating with me about the value in things like self-sufficient toileting was not easy. This tested and challenged them professionally because they had to help me look beyond my insecurities.

I had never been taken to the bathroom by anyone other than family and had to watch myself struggling to eat at home. Resenting strangers invading my privacy, I did my best to avoid participating in these group activities. During lunch at the center, I tried to face the others in the kitchen. It nauseated me to see their grotesquely familiar table manners and strange eating habits.

Watching others slobbering their food and leaving a trail of crumbs, wet paper, chunks of uneaten food on the table or floor, and pieces of half-eaten food on their clothing made me sick. It is not pleasant to watch a person with cerebral palsy continually stab at a plate of food until it becomes a disgusting mass of ooze. I saw a mirror of myself, and that hurt.

Toileting was difficult because it was strange to make a group activity out of such a private and personal affair. Help had never been easy to accept before, even when my family was offering the assistance. Though I dreaded the thought of wetting my clothing, I preferred it to having a stranger invade the most private areas of my body. With or without assistance, the entire ordeal took about forty-five minutes. Embarrassed and ashamed at my lack of self-control, this was one of the most trying times in my young adulthood.

Because my struggles with the bathroom ritual caused such distress, I learned to compensate by cutting back on foods and liquids while at the center. I sought to avoid conflict by eliminating the need to use the bathroom until I was back home. I remember going home on the bus in physical agony, wetting myself when it became an emergency. The whole bus knew that smell, and I hated my inability to assert control over the situation.

Although I did not enjoy being treated like a child, I still behaved like one whenever Jane, Bettye, and I entered into a confrontation over my eating or toileting. It was almost a full year before I made an honest effort to cooperate. It took Jane and Bettye showing me the pride I could feel in accomplishing these things, kind of the same philosophy Uncle Nora used, before I found courage to tackle these obstacles. Funny that it took many trials and errors with the same conclusion, more independence, before I saw feeding and toileting myself in the same light as beating Peter in a game of chess.

Once I caught on to the secret of how personal hygiene and feeding myself made me feel, it became addictive. I refused to use the adapted utensils they suggested, considering it a sign of weakness. To me, using adapted utensils further reinforces the concept of "handicapism." I won't even use them today. With a great deal of effort and many hours of practice, I mastered the art of using regular utensils to eat. Once the staff understood my desire to avoid appearing more disabled than I actually was, they were more than willing to allow my input in teaching and guiding me.

It was nearly three years, though, before I could use the bathroom without experiencing the same pain and discomfort I once did. Peter was very supportive of me during this time, encouraging me to accept help, not because I should appreciate it, but because I needed it. Eventually, I allowed the presence of a helper during the toileting procedure. I learned with more practice to manage with virtual independence. This put me and everyone else at the center more at ease.

We were all trying to adjust to the demands and realistic expectations of our individualized programming objectives. Adjustment meant becoming a tight-knit community, instead of isolated people in pursuit of narrow goals. As time progressed, with the patience and support of Dr. Holder and her staff, we recognized the need to look beyond the parameters of our collective disabilities and perspectives. We learned to function jointly toward a perspective shared by friends and classmates, albeit different in various ways, with the singular dream of independent living. This was my first real introduction to the power and effectiveness of teamwork between various structures of diverse associations of people who seek to overcome shared and common problems.

Dr. Holder brought a variety of visitors to the center: professional people, college students, parents, friends, and other members of the larger community. We learned to prepare for and greet a variety of different guests. As they asked questions, Dr. Holder encouraged us to answer based on our personal and collective experiences. We all benefited from this. The visitors, especially the college students, gained useful insight concerning our lifestyles and exceptionalities.

We were not perfect, nor were we always willing to compromise and make sacrifices as a group. Exposed to a variety of different experimental teaching styles as Dr. Holder's graduate students finished their requirements for graduation, we all learned to teach and be taught by others. I found it important to approach every new person or experience with an open mind. I also discovered how much better I saw the weaknesses in my own points of view by learning what other people thought about disabilities.

I learned to be more assertive, and for the first time in my life, I felt a calling. The more I heard about the growing need for political representation of disabled needs by the disabled, the more I felt that I had to do something. I met Barbara Cotter, an employee of Alabama Disabilities Advocacy Program, in the spring of 1975. Our relationship would later have a tremendous impact on my life and work in Alabama.

Mary Jo Deaver was a beautiful example of one vibrant volunteer at the center. We developed a spiritual bond through music therapy and the talks we shared. From the moment she first came into my presence, there was a literal burst of creative energy between us. She taught me to truly appreciate music of all types, and thoughtful lyrics over entertaining nonsense. Mary Jo shared complex compositions of music and poetry with us, and they were the most inspiring art some of us at the center had ever experienced.

I have developed a taste for Chopin and the Russian composer Sergei Rachmaninoff. Hank Williams Jr. or John Lee Hooker will soothe the soul on a lonely summer night, as much as George Clinton or Bela Fleck and the Flecktones will lift the spirits. From Earth, Wind, and Fire to Widespread Panic, Seal to Sting, Lauryn Hill to Ani DiFranco, and Ben Harper to Bob Dylan, my tastes in modern music vary tremendously. The more music of the world I listen to, the more I can appreciate, and the better in touch I feel with the human spirit.

Mary Jo encouraged us to believe in ourselves. Although Uncle and I discussed the importance of God, it was she who allowed me to recognize gifts from God of my own. From this extraordinary lady, I learned the value of prayer and its power to affect my life. Mary Jo's friendship was an instrumental part of my education, both as a student and human being. I thank God for the miracle she performed in my life and is still doing today as a gifted teacher in the Birmingham public school system. Some teachers are born, not made.

Peter, Snow, Frank, and I became a family of caring adults, drawing strength from one another. West Alabama Comprehensive Services (WACS) was created for all of us, not just the disabled. It was conceived with the hope that given the proper tools, even the severely physically challenged could make a useful contribution to American life. Dr. Holder and teachers like Mary Jo inspired us with the goal of becoming contributors to society instead of burdens. When the center was formally dedicated in 1980, Peter used his literary eloquence to capture the quintessential spirit of WACS inthe follwing document.

> The design of the *WACS Crest* was completed in 1980 by Mark Singer, then resident counselor at WACS. The staff and clients felt that we should have a symbol to signify to ourselves and others what the WACS Program means to us.

The wheelchair represents independence for all disabled people. It is the way people with multiple disabilities are able to move about in this world. At WACS we are challenged to be as independent as possible and are encouraged to experience life in its fullness. When I first got my electric wheelchair, it was an open door to all kinds of possibilities. Right now, technology has not advanced to the point where there is a better substitute for a wheelchair. I hope someday there will be a form of transportation available for disabled individuals that does not have the stereotype that goes along with the wheelchair such as: mentally retarded, pitiful, or disgusting. The symbol of the wheelchair gives us hope that when plans are being made for any public building or service, no one will close the door to us again by constructing buildings with curbs, stairs, and doors that we cannot open. It is also a reminder that ultimately we must assume responsibility for ourselves.

The clasped hands signify the unity we have and the willingness to lend a helping hand. There is not a group of people anywhere that are more willing to help each other in a brotherly way. WACS has been a family for those who have none, a brother for the brotherless, a sister for the sisterless. There is a true and sincere family feeling among the clients. We have grown with each other. We all feel a sense of accomplishment when any one of us triumphs.

The symbol of the dove represents peace and hope. Hope is something that disabled people don't talk about much. We don't dare discuss it because we don't want to throw ourselves into an anxious state. There are many opportunities available to disabled individuals, so we at WACS don't have much time to spend hoping for miracles. We are more involved with moving toward a successful life with what we have. But we trust that someday, however far in the future, there will be that twinkling star of hope that is symbolized through the dove. Undoubtedly, it is the same hope that Noah prayed for when coming into a new life in a clean, new world.

The symbol of the heart and flaming candle represents the love and dedication we have for each other and the people who have helped us over the years. Love is usually something that is

> difficult to talk about. We at WACS understand each others' problems so well that we feel more than sympathy for each other. By sensing each others' needs and experiencing each others' problems, we have developed true love for one another. The burning candle represents personal insight and growth that may be gained through this love.

I learned many skills at WACS that have guided me toward a life filled with realistic and attainable goals. I still have run-ins with uninformed individuals who would talk to me in the third person, as if with an attendant present I cease to be part of a conversation about my own interests. It took me many years to develop this type of savvy, and after setting them straight we are both the better for it. WACS helped me through some difficult times. I owe much to the program and I am indebted to the staff for the tools they equipped me with.

The first of its kind in my state, West Alabama Comprehensive Services expanded in 1988 to accommodate more students. They represent the wheelchair, clasped hands, dove, and heart and flaming candle, as the WACS crest is still in use today. The original building at 14 Thomas Circle was vacated and torn down. The new building is behind the VA hospital in Tuscaloosa. It is here that my love of education was kindled, and I is first introduced to the eccentric breadth of humanity known as college students.

Building a Dream

Besides Peter, Frank, and Snow, I had four new classmates my first year at the Adult Work Activity Center: Wilma Clark, Brenda Gravett, Jerry Mitchell, and Betty Dooley. An Individualized Education Plan (IEP) was developed for the new students, similar to ours but modified to encompass each student's full abilities. My IEP included reading at the top, because at twenty I was reading little more than street signs. I was still working on the basics of feeding myself and going to the bathroom alone as well. We were all working on our etiquette and developing survival skills like using a telephone book or dictionary, and reading the newspaper to keep up with current events.

Jane Shaw was proud of our accomplishments. I never learned to write at Northington, but now, thanks to her, I was learning to write my name. We were making arts and crafts, even Christmas decorations. Still, Jane felt that something was missing. Besides swimming, which we did once a week at the university's indoor pool, we needed some other kind of recreational activity.

Jane had been searching for a recreational outlet for some time when she read in a United Cerebral Palsy (UCP) newsletter of a UCP- and Special Olympics–sponsored regional bowling tournament in Atlanta. Jane described it to us, explaining that we would be using a ramp designed to allow us better control over the ball. We were overwhelmingly in favor of participating. While we discussed what our group's name might be, she filled out the attached application.

Everyone had an idea of what we should call ourselves. After three days of discussion, the Bama Bombers and the Bama Tenpinners were two names that seemed to have the most support. A vote was in order. We cast our ballots, and the Bama Tenpinners it was, winning by a slight majority. Jane sent off our application.

While waiting for notification of our acceptance to participate in the tournament, Jane, Bettye, and Dr. Holder began, with Bobby Wyatt and Howard Hinesly, to prepare us for going out in public. This trip was to be our first outing ever and every one of us, excluding Peter, was socially uncouth, to say the least. In fact, we had no idea how to face the public or what to expect. The social aspects of our lives had been limited until this point, and the staff at the center had their hands full.

First, we had many group discussions. The staff listened avidly and answered our questions realistically. We began to realize what had to be done, as Jane described what our trip would entail. Teamwork was the key to victory, to our social education, to our overall success.

We worked rigorously on learning the basics, including table manners, social graces, proper speech (we all cussed like sailors), and how to support each other should one of us get in trouble. We developed a buddy system to ensure that no one would be left alone in a potentially stressful or dangerous situation. Jane and Bettye supported us unconditionally. They gave us a sense of belonging and the chance to compete on our own level.

Our acceptance notification came in about two weeks, and we began learning to bowl. With a month until the tournament, we had to whip ourselves into shape. Twice a week we went down to Leland Lanes, the local alley, to practice. Spiller Furniture of Tuscaloosa sponsored our cause by printing white golf shirts with "Bama Tenpinners" on the back and our names on the front. We felt like an official team and took our bowling lessons very seriously.

With one week left until our Atlanta trip, the training schedule intensified. We assessed our collective strengths and deficits. Peter, Wilma, and I were the best of our group in actual bowling skills, but Snow was dynamic. He challenged each of us to do our best. By the time we left for the tournament, the Bama Tenpinners were smoking, and we knew it.

The only word I can think of to describe the regional tournament is landslide! We blew everybody away. There were representative teams from Alabama, Tennessee, Mississippi, Louisiana, Georgia, and Kentucky, to name a few. Peter bowled 206, setting a new tournament record, as he took the all-around Best Male Bowler award. Wilma bowled 186, taking the award for all-around Best Female Bowler. I didn't do too shabbily either, bowling 169 for the third-highest score on the team. We were ecstatic! On to the National UCP Bowling Tournament!

The national competition was scheduled for April in New Orleans. That gave us less than a month, and we needed all the time we could get to prepare. Jane, Bettye, and Dr. Holder warned us against overconfidence. They thought we would get cocky, but nothing could be further from the truth. We were all extremely nervous and willing to work harder than ever to ensure our victory and make Jane even more proud than she was already. We doubled our time at Leland Lanes, increasing from two to four times a week; the Bama Tenpinners owned New Orleans.

After the speeding ticket we received on the way down (which didn't sit well with the university, let me tell you), we checked into the Marriott Hotel in New Orleans on the evening of April 16, 1974 amidst a flurry of activity. We didn't care. We were in New Orleans! Jane had promised to introduce us to the wild side of the famous southern seaport and give us a historical tour. Nobody cared about history. We wanted Bourbon Street! Our pleas were ignored all the way to the hotel.

Vans were unloading participants out front. The lobby was filled with people with every kind of cerebral palsy in existence: walking to and fro, wheeling themselves about, walking with crutches. It was a bit intimidating, but we were electrified. There were teams consisting of combined residents from forty-five or so states in attendance, and we were determined to beat them all.

That first night, we went out to sample the local flavor, and did we ever! From the bars on Bourbon Street to various seafood establishments along the pier, we partied until the midnight hour with a smorgasbord of strangers. The Cajun food was spicy and delicious, the jazz was kicking, and the girls looked ravishing. With the help of our attendants, Peter and I managed to sneak a few drinks, unbeknownst to Bettye and Jane. None of us had ever witnessed the craziness that makes New Orleans famous, and it was a blast!

Wilma, however, wasn't feeling well. She had been ill since we left Tuscaloosa and now had a slight temperature. She was quivering with excitement about the competition, though, and determined not to let down the team. She refused to talk about it, failing to mention how sick she actually felt.

The next day started at five in the morning. None of us could really sleep that night. There was a certain air about the whole tournament. This was going to be exhilarating for all of us, the most important effort each of us had ever made. For some of us, like Wilma and myself, this was a real chance to be the best at something. Unlike those Northington softball games, here was a contest where our skills were tested on an equal level with our peers from across the entire country.

For Wilma, this was the most important moment of her life. She saw the tournament as a once-in-a-lifetime opportunity to really do something, her chance to shine. She had discovered over the last few months that she was an exceptional bowler, one of the best in the country. She held the female title in the Southeast and was bent on being the best in the nation.

Wilma had myelomeningocele, the severest form of spina bifida. She had no feeling from the waist down, and her kidneys were no longer functioning. Without pain, Wilma had no way of determining how ill she actually was. She had a catheter which entered her side and emptied her bodily waste into a sanitary bag attached to the side of her wheelchair. Her illness was therefore carefully watched by Bettye and Jane, regardless of her attempts to shun concern.

The warm-up trials began at seven o'clock. There were sixteen teams, consisting of representative members from almost every state in the continental United States. The first round began at eight o'clock that morning and lasted until six o'clock that evening. It was a fierce competition, eliminating all but five teams by the day's end.

The Bama Tenpinners were magnificent! Through serious play, we managed to score high enough to qualify. The first day's round eliminated all but five teams, and the second left four. A team out of Ohio had outscored us, and held the top cumulative score going into the finals. We realized that everyone here meant business. This was not going to be as easy as Atlanta. In order to win, we had to utilize the utmost limits of our skill; if we were going to be number one, the Bama Tenpinners would have to bowl that way.

Before each day, Wilma passed out a special perfumed oil we smeared on our foreheads for luck. Wilma, Frank, Snow, Peter, and I had an outstanding two days. Frank had scores of 135 and 148 respectively, while Snow had a 159 and a 167. Peter and Wilma were outstanding, tying in the first round with 192. In the second Peter had a 198 and Wilma had a 189. I came in behind Snow with a 143 on the first day and a 163 on the second day.

Throughout the second day of tournament play, Wilma's condition worsened. She hotly protested as Bettye and Jane rushed her to a New Orleans hospital. After a cursory examination, the emergency room doctor told Wilma what she already suspected:

"Miss Clark, you have developed an infection of the urinary tract. This is caused by the catheter controlling your waste elimination. The infection has been there for some time and must have immediate attention. You don't have long to live."

As Jane called Dr. Holder, Wilma pleaded with Bettye, "Please, you've got to let me play. This is the most important time in my life. Please, you must let me play."

"Wilma, you realize the risks involved are too great to allow . . ."

"All the same reasons for allowing me to finish the tournament. The team needs me, and besides, the Bama Tenpinners will be disqualified if I cannot continue. You know that as well as I, and I refuse to let down my team or myself! Now, out of my way! I have a tournament to win."

Jane and Bettye got the message she was trying to convey. The rest of us knew that something had been amiss. When she returned to the hotel room, we understood what had to be done. The Bama Tenpinners had to win, for the sake of Wilma and for ourselves. She was the most magically inspiring person in our lives, and I promised to do everything within my power to ensure our victory.

We came onto the alley with steely determination and tenacity that morning. Each member was fully aware of the situation. Bowling with a vengeance, we blew away the first team, from Massachusetts. As the final round with the team from Ohio approached, we realized victory was within our grasp. Wilma reminded us that it was crucial we make every ball count.

We rocked their world, outscoring Ohio by a remarkable ninety-seven points. Wilma bowled an unbelievable 206, setting a new UCP National Bowling Tournament women's record. Jane and Bettye were astonished! Wilma was our hero, leading the team to victory. It wasn't over yet, though. The winner was not determined by the team with the most victories, it was the team with the most cumulative points. This was to be revealed at a luncheon immediately following the final round of play.

Bettye took Wilma up to the hotel room to rest before the trip back. She stayed with Wilma, while the rest of the team went with Jane into the Marriott ballroom to celebrate. Tension mounted as the announcement came of the new National Champions. When we heard Wilma Clark's name announced for Overall Best Female, we knew that the championship was in the bag. As we yelled and applauded, Jane accepted Wilma's award in her absence.

The Bama Tenpinners were declared the new National Champions! We were ecstatic! Jane found a phone and called Bettye up in the room to tell Wilma of her achievement. When she heard about her award, Wilma broke into tears, as the realization of a dream unfolded before her eyes. Congratulatory telegrams arrived from Governor of Alabama, George C. Wallace, and Lieutenant Governor Jere Beasley.

After the luncheon, we packed up to leave. On the way to our van, a blue limousine pulled up. As a beautiful lady emerged from inside, Peter yelled, "Hey! Isn't that Gladys Knight? It is! Hey y'all! That's Gladys Knight and the Pips!" Jane introduced herself, and told them of our victory.

Gladys came over and offered her congratulations. She tried to give us free tickets to her concert that night, but unfortunately we had to decline. Wilma was getting sicker by the minute. She needed medical attention as soon as we could get her home.

Bettye and our attendant staff rode in a car that followed the van. Wilma tried to join in the celebration but was unable due to the severity of her illness. We encouraged her to hang on as long as she could until we could get her home. She reached way down in her soul for the strength to make it. Once we arrived back in Tuscaloosa, Wilma was taken home to her family, where they were informed of her dire need. They took her to Druid City Hospital, where she passed away three days later.

Dr. Holder stayed with Wilma and offered loving support during those desperate hours before her death. Jane came in the next morning with tears running down her face. Peter sadly whispered, "She's gone." Wilma Clark died on April 21, 1974, champion, teammate, and close friend. I will always remember her fighting spirit. She taught me never to give up on anything I do, to see it through from start to finish.

New Challenges

We missed Wilma. Everyone at the center was, in some way or other, touched by her presence. Yet, there was no time for mourning, as our schedules did not leave any room for being depressed. After the bowling tournament, we began preparations for another exciting event, a two-week field trip to Camp Challenge.

Founded in 1961 by the Easter Seal Society, Camp Challenge is situated about thirty miles outside of Orlando, Florida, in a town called Sorrento. The camp's intention is to provide recreational facilities in an outdoor atmosphere geared to meet the special needs of the disabled. With sixty-three acres of land in a rustic setting, it is an ideal environment for personal growth. In addition, parents and disabled children get a needed summer vacation away from one another.

Through class discussion Jane and the staff laid out the groundwork for our trip. We participated in preparatory activities, which incorporated every aspect of camp life. After three weeks of intense work, we boarded a bus and left for Camp Challenge on May 17, 1974. The trip took an exhausting fourteen hours, and I remember vividly how badly I had to use the bathroom. I held it during the entire trip, and by the time I got off of that horrendous bus and into the appropriate facility, I had nearly wet myself. What a symphonic release that was!

We were taken into the dining hall for supper with about ninety other campers of all ages. After a hearty meal, we were given cabin assignments that were separated by gender. Peter and I ended up together. "Somebody messed up, Nate," he whispered devilishly in my ear, "We gonna have us a good time here!" There wasn't time for tricks that first night; everyone was way too tired from the drive. We unloaded our baggage and went to bed.

Over the next two weeks, we engaged in a wide variety of activities. You would be surprised to learn about the multitude of things people with severe disabilities are capable of. During the day we went swimming, fishing, boating, and even hiking! We made arts and crafts, learned basic riflery and archery, and played many sports including basketball, baseball, and elementary girl watching. The latter, of course, being my personal favorite. At night we built bonfires, roasted hot dogs and marshmallows, told ghost stories, and goofed off.

The group of us had several serious talks. Late at night by the poolside we discussed God and religions, politics, girls, our individual disabilities, and how much progress we each had made toward becoming independent and spiritually whole. Under the starlit Florida sky, Peter and I strengthened our friendship. We made a pact that we would always be there for one another throughout our lives and that through thick and thin we would strive toward greatness in each and every endeavor.

Crazy schemes filled Peter's head as we readied for bed each night. He came up with some great pranks and enlisted my help in carrying them out. One night, with the help of our attendants, we filled a bucket to the rim with, shall we say, various and sundry types of yellow-golden liquid. Positioning it above the entryway into our cabin, we feverishly awaited the arrival of our intended victim, Ms. Jane Shaw! She came up the pathway to say good night and was about to open the door, when we burst out into a fit of uncontrollable giggling. She realized something was fishy and caught on to our little booby trap. We had foiled our own gross ploy!

The next morning Jane got even. We were all eating at the breakfast table when she nonchalantly strolled up to Peter and me with a fiendish grin on her face. "Remember last night? Well, I have a little surprise for you two." She gradually edged my chair out from the table and began to push me toward the door. With the pool in view and approaching rapidly, I yelped and cried out, realizing exactly what kind of surprise I had in store. Splash! I laughed and spit water as my clothes got soaking wet. She threw Peter in later that day, but laughing the loudest as usual, I got it first.

Camp Challenge also opened new romantic doors for me. During our free time in the afternoons, all the campers would lie out in the big orange grove behind the dining hall. There, we would eat oranges and other fruits while getting to know each other intimately. I had my eye on one girl named Bonnie. She was an intoxicating beauty from Minnesota, and I badgered her from the moment we first met. We got closer the second night, and I guess you could say that our flower bloomed, but I'll leave the details to your imagination.

At the end of the first week, on Friday, Jane took the whole group to Orlando for a free tour of Walt Disney World. We were all glad to have the chance to go. I saw many sights: parades, cartoon characters from different films, immense buildings, and massive commercialism. The only letdown was that none of us could ride anything daring. I wanted to get on the Wild West roller coaster ride or go 2000 Leagues Under the Sea, but we were limited in time, so the Small, Small World boat ride was the extent of our adventuring that afternoon. "I'll be back, and next time I will ride them all," I swore to myself.

We had a banquet on the last night, where each of us received awards for perseverance and accomplishment. I won an award for holding my breath underwater longer than anyone else. I learned camping outdoors that there was more to life than just being cooped up inside all the time. Natural beauty, combined with all the seemingly impossible things I was able to do, gave me a greater appreciation of my capabilities instead of causing me to feel weighted down with my disability.

In October of 1974 Mary Jo Deaver and I took an introductory course in the brand-new techniques of Silva Mind Control. It was held on the University of Alabama campus at the Continuing Education building. I wanted to perfect the meditation skills Uncle Nora had already begun to teach me in hopes that I would continue to gain more control over my body. I had exaggerated expectations, of course, wanting Silva Mind Control to be a cure-all for cerebral palsy. With a name like that, what should I have expected? My brother Milton was quick to point out that he "didn't believe in that nonsense," reminding me that I should be skeptical as well.

Our instructor, Mr. Ed Tunure, led the classes skillfully. He impressed me with the need to confront myself honestly and realistically. The course helped me to use mental exertion for more creative problem solving and improved my meditation skills. I practiced the exercises I learned with Uncle Nora. Milton was delighted to hear the classes were helpful in guiding me toward a more positive attitude about my disability.

During the fall of 1974, Milton played as a linebacker on County High School's varsity football team. I went to see him play a few times. He had grown large and muscular during his high school years. Milton had many girlfriends and one steady girlfriend. There's a complicated story behind those two I'll address later. Milton loved me very much, and I remember the fun we used to have.

He wanted me to participate in neighborhood activities and would organize weekend checkers tournaments. Together we would challenge the boys, including longtime friends like Tommy Bostic. After our games we would sit around and drink homemade cherry wine from the gathered fruits of our nearby tree. Those were good times before his graduation in May of 1975. The following summer was no exception.

Despite all the time we spent together, something was eating at Milton. He assured me that nothing was wrong, but he was inexplicably restless. I knew he had big dreams and elaborate plans of his own. Milton was always talking to me about doing great things with my life, just as he planned the same with his. He would tell me what was bothering him when the time was right, and I had faith in his ability to make decisions.

Earlier that same year, I had come home from the center one day and announced, "Momma, I want to take the GED I heard about it from my teacher."

"What is dat GED? Do you know, Milton?"

"The GED is an equivalent to a high school diploma. A lot of people get their high school diploma, Momma."

"That's well an' fine Milton, but Nathan, he handicapped. He is jus' wastin' his time. He don't need no education. An education ain't gonna help him."

"Momma, why won't an education help him? He's just like everybody else. Nathan is smart in more ways then we are. He can remember stuff that we tell him, and he can think for his own self, so why won't an education help him?"

"Milton, you got to realize dat he cain't walk, an' fillin' his head wit' all of dem dreams is jus' gonna make him more uncontrollable than he is now. People like dat, dey don't have no reason fo' an education."

"B . . . But Momma, I need my education so I can take care of myself when you leave me, 'cause you ain't always gonna be here to take care of me. Ten, f . . . fifteen years from now, if you die, who gonna take care of me then?"

"Boy, dat's nonsense you talkin'. If I die, yo' brothers an' sisters will take care of you."

"Momma, why can't chou undestan' dat dey have lives of their own, an' dey ain't gonna have time to take care of me?"

"He right, Momma. We ain't gonna have time to take care of Nathan. Nathan is perfectly capable of learning to take care of his own self."

"Dat boy cain't take care of hisself, Milton. He cain't feed hisself, and he cain't even take hisself to de bathroom. Now tell me, boy, how you figure he gonna ever live on his own?"

"A lot of crippled folks do. They have a program called 'Rehabilitation.' A representative from the West Alabama Rehabilitation Center (WARC) came and spoke to our class about different career opportunities available to people like Nathan or those who wish to work with him."

"That is for folks who kin use dere arms. Nathan cain't even control his own arms, Milton."

"They have special equipment that will allow Nathan to do things without using his arms. You would be surprised."

Afterwards, under the cherry tree, Milton and I had a long talk about examining the consequences of my future choices and actions. Then he looked around us. In a hushed tone, he voiced some shocking news, "I have a secret to share with you, Nate. I'm leaving soon, to enlist in the United States Marine Corps, and you are gonna have to be strong. I want to see the world; there's so much of it out there just waiting to be explored. If you work diligently, and really apply yourself, this dream of yours will come true. I believe in you, Nathan, because I know you have potential, but most importantly because I love you."

I was a little scared by the news, but had kind of expected him to tell me something along those lines. At that point, I determined to get myself an education no matter how long or tedious the road ahead. I resolved to look into this rehabilitation thing. If I could get involved in the program, perhaps I could do something constructive like get a job and an apartment. Besides, I didn't want to live at home anymore, not if Milton was leaving. It was time for another chat with Dr. Holder.

On My Own

On my twenty-first birthday, in June of 1975, I became ineligible for Crippled Children's Services. I was no longer receiving physical therapy or any other services from them and had not been since the opening of the center in Tuscaloosa. I had to be labeled as EMR, or "educable mentally retarded" before I could be accepted under the entry criteria for the Adult Work Activity Center. The federal grant Dr. Holder received did not cover people with unique, non-mentally-disabling conditions.

Although I didn't realize it at the time, the "educable mentally retarded" label posed many problems for my future growth. This label is applied earlier than ever to a wider range of minority children today. How so many children can be described as brain damaged before they are given a chance to learn anything confuses and astounds me. It is almost as if we want to convince certain American children that by virtue of class and birthright they are to be assigned roles suitable, even within public education, to a subservient station in life! Labeling children this way, and then expecting them to be motivated to find jobs and other meaningful ways to contibute to society, is a recipe for social suicide.

The future for disabled adult education and job training was, and remains, very limited. I decided, being twenty-one, that the time had come for me to spread my wings a little further. Vocational training was available at the West Alabama Rehabilitation Center in Tuscaloosa. I encountered difficulty in receiving consideration, though, due to my specific disability. Most professionals within the rehabilitation system feel that cerebral palsy is a nonmarketable disabling condition. This is also true of rehabilitation services at state universities across this country. More so now than ever before.

I maintain that individuals with cerebral palsy and other developmental or progressive disabilities and labels are rarely given a fair shake at the education which can place them, if nowhere else, within the teaching profession. We live in a scary world today. It seems if you are very ill, disabled, poor, growing but unborn, elderly, or considered nonmarketable by "market forces," then the value of your life and work, the distribution of your opportunity, can be limited and called into question. Worth of an individual cannot be established by pure marketability any more than the value of art can be tallied and categorically determined. Who knows, and can state with any true authority, how a child will learn and grow, who should live and die, or when the market and what it values may change?

History is full of examples of humanity's technological advances and business sense far outweighing its conventional wisdom. The planet is an ecological mess, opportunity for the culturally disadvantaged has become a political war of nerves, and America has no shame. I know that severely disabled individuals have much to contribute to addressing major problems, and their contributions lie in their ability to incorporate things like patience, and virtues gleaned from delayed gratification within their philosophizing, organizing, writing, planning, and solving. Give a severely disabled individual the proper tools, and they can share a world of information, supplemented by the wisdom of their experience, their love of personal freedom, and the strength of their character.

Camp Challenge had given me a taste of freedom my spirit yearned for. As conflicts grew both at home and with my teachers at the center, especially in light of the forthcoming tremendous loss of major support from Milton, I began to question the need for my dependence on anyone at all. Entrusted with my brother's secret, I had a hard time explaining a desire to be self-reliant and out of the house, without giving too much away.

Dr. Holder, Jane, and Beth all agreed that I deserved the opportunity to enter the rehabilitation system on a trial basis. They merely wanted me to understand that I needed training in areas of specific skills before I would be able to achieve even partially independent living. Milton pushed Momma in my direction daily until he left us. She was dead set against my involvement in any such program, based on her limited perspective.

Uncle Nora understood her overprotective nature. He gently persuaded her in my direction, while simultaneously showing me the wisdom of her position and that of the staff at the center.

"Son, I undestan' your concern about de future. You got to realize, Nathan, dat God didn't build de Earth in one day. Folks will always treat you in a abnormal way when you try to convince 'em of what you is thinkin', as dey done me, until I realized dat knowledge of yo'self and of yo' environment plays an important part in achievin' your goals in life. I'm not sayin' you are wrong for takin' de position you've taken, but you need help to express it de best way. You are tryin' to climb a damn mountain too steep fo' you to climb right now. Mountain climbers often get a better idea of what dey is climbing before dey go up one an' dat is what you gotta do."

I heard Uncle's words, but the gravity of his message did not sink in. I pretended to agree with him, in order to ensure his help in convincing Momma. Having a marketable trade, I thought, would give me an identity and a future. Following months of heated debate and discussion with Dr. Holder, we agreed to a fair compromise. I was to enter West Alabama

Rehabilitation Center on January 13, 1976, by agreeing to spend half days in rehabilitation training and the other half at the center.

The marines uphold every ideal that my brother admired: courage, strength, endurance, leadership, responsibility and self-discipline. He announced his departure on the very day he planned to leave: November 25, 1975. The entire household remained flabbergasted as he caught a Greyhound to the Birmingham USMC recruiting station. When Momma begged him not to go, he merely said, "I have to do this; it is my dream, Momma. Try to understand this. I love y'all, but I have to look towards the future, and mine is bigger than Northport, Alabama."

Milton signed for a four-year tour in the Ground Field Subprogram Combat Support Z-1. He went through basic training at Camp Le Jeune in North Carolina, after which he was transferred to Parris Island. It wasn't long before Momma's anger dissipated into melancholy. Milton was her favorite and everyone knew it. I was overjoyed to hear that things were going well for him, but I had my hands full in preparation for my own trials that were about to begin.

Immediately upon entry into the Rehabilitation Center, I faced a battery of vocational tests, including some requiring me to perform tasks of intricate fine motor skills using one or both hands. Never taking into account the need for manual skills that were testable for realistic employment, I had also refused to recognize that most jobs require some knowledge of the ability to read and write. Although I struggled with it for nearly three months, without these skills I was unable to make an adequate adjustment to their program.

I had a completely different idea of what rehabilitation was supposed to entail, figuring it would resemble life at the center. It was actually like a job in many respects. I would get dropped off after lunch on a bus from WACS and go clock in my time card, after which I went to an assembly line where I placed nuts and bolts into boxes for about forty-five minutes. Further down, the boxes were taped and shipped to the loading zone, where trucks picked them up for delivery to a variety of local business establishments.

After an hour of pitifully excersizing my feeble manual dexterity, and scattering nuts and bolts all over the assembly line in a poor attempt to aim them into boxes passing me constantly, I would quit in frustration. They could see I was trying, but my cerebral palsy would cause me to miss the boxes every time. The more determined I became, the more my stress level would rise, and my spasms and vocal interruption would in turn increase accordingly. The supervisor would say to me in consternation, "You are more trouble than you are worth."

I completed the evaluation phases of programming and placement assessments at West Alabama Easter Seal Rehabilitation Center and was turned down on March 8, 1976: "limited or no vocational potential." I was referred to the local Vocational Rehabilitation Service for three more months of testing and evaluation. Although I redoubled my efforts to complete their requirements, I was turned down again.

Hurt, depressed, and filled with bitterness, for the first time since the parallel bar fiasco, I felt like a total failure. I began to revert back to some of the less than noble aspects of my personality. Denial became my game, one that I had played very well in the past, and one that I could pull off with a definite degree of skill. I drew strength from my creative imagination, and set out to convince the world that despite what anyone else thought, Nathan Ballard was A-OK.

The only person I fooled was myself. I was far from okay, and Dr. Holder, Beth, and Uncle Nora knew it. The more I blamed everyone else, the less they would let me escape the fact that only I could make my life better or worse. My fighting spirit was undaunted, and the staff at the center were careful to guide me toward a clearer reality without dampening my enthusiasm. Uncle Nora preferred a less subtle approach.

"Boy, dis game you playin' ain't no use. What would yo' brother Milton say if he could see you now? Boy, it's about time you realized, dere ain't nobody gonna help you but yo'self. If you don't stop kidding yo'self into believin' Nathan Ballard is some kind of Superman, you gonna find the world is a very harsh place."

"What are you sayin' Uncle? D . . . Dat I cain't do it? Dat I cain't get me a job an' git out from under Momma's damn wing?"

"All I'm tellin' you is dis, you gotta take it one step at a time."

Eventually I woke up to what everyone around me was trying to get across. West Alabama Rehabilitation Center was merely another barrier to overcome, another group to prove wrong. Sue Hoggle, my counselor at WARC, believed in me and suggested another alternative. There was a rehabilitation facility in Birmingham called Lakeshore that perhaps had other options in careers for the disabled than working on an assembly line. She sent them my file with a cover letter explaining her feeling that I deserved another chance.

At her request, an interview was arranged for the afternoon of April 13, 1976. I went home from the center on that afternoon of good news with fiery confidence. Lakeshore was ahead, and my prospects were growing. "This time," I told myself, "nothing can hold me down. I'm gonna kick ass and take names!"

PART TWO

The Tumultuous Path

Climbing the Mountain

In August of 1975, I had been asked to serve as the United Cerebral Palsy poster adult in my district. This included the counties of Tuscaloosa, Bibb, Pickens, Chilton, Fayette, and the rest of West Alabama. Photographs of me were taken in August and September at the local TV station. On September 10 and 11, during the Regional Telethon, my classmates and I were interviewed on television discussing the Adult Work Activity Center, its benefit to our lives, and the pulse of our community. This was my first introduction to work for UCP, and it opened the door of opportunity to my future career as a spokesperson and advocate for the disabled.

Jane Shaw left us that October to marry a disabled man named Steve Maples. Beth Bruden became our second full-time teacher, while Bettye Roberts remained on staff as her assistant. I told Mary Jo about Lakeshore and she was delighted about the possibility of my entering their transitional living unit. I had my hopes up when the initial meetings were arranged.

Sue suggested a long-term placement of eighteen months at Lakeshore for special skills instruction. Sue, Dr. Holder, Mary Jo, and Beth spent time in consultation determining where my skills could be used most effectively. Despite the limited range of motion in my arms, they felt that I would be better suited to train in the areas of microfilming or computer programming. As it turns out, Lakeshore had also anticipated similar training and placement objectives.

In the meantime, I began hassling the staff at the center about my desire to take the GED and learn to read better. As I anticipated, no one was very enthusiastic about the idea at first. They all felt that trying to get me into a rehabilitation program was difficult enough. Besides, I could hardly read and write, much less take a written exam. I let it be, at least for the time being, but I told Beth and Dr. Holder they should seriously consider my idea.

On the Tuesday before leaving, everyone at the center threw a farewell party in my honor. Saying goodbye proved to be much more difficult than I anticipated. "Good luck! I hope you make it, my friend," was all Peter could manage to say, then he wheeled himself away. As Dr. Holder hugged me before I left, I momentarily had second thoughts. I was about to leave my closest friends and family, and though I felt like I had it together, in the face of change a part of me wanted to remain in these familiar surroundings forever. Nonetheless, Lakeshore was an exciting prospect, and I tearfully bade them farewell.

Later that night, I dealt with the family. Most everyone was very proud of me, saying I should "make the best of the opportunity." Momma helped me pack my things together, and she even seemed a bit more enthusiastic than usual. Auntie and Uncle Nora gave me their own last minute advice before bed. The next morning, after loading up the trunk, Momma, Ray, Annie Bell, Nora, and myself all piled into Auntie's white 1965 Cadillac and headed over to Birmingham.

My heart pounded as we drove up the long circular driveway of the facility, and signs of spring everywhere filled me with hope for the future. Uncle Nora lifted me out of the car, and together we went inside. Near Red Mountain, Lakeshore resembles a resort with cottages nestled into a natural backdrop. The secretary at the front desk announced my presence, and we waited together for Dr. Trough to call me back. After a cursory physical examination, the doctor quietly asked Momma to remove me from the room, then she went inside and conversed with him for about thirty minutes behind closed doors.

They came out together and the doctor stated, "Nathan, you would be better off at the facility you are at now." My picture of a pleasant place, where even disabled adults from poor backgrounds could find sanctuary, evaporated before my eyes. How could this be? Had someone played a nasty trick on me?

I asked Uncle Nora, "This is a joke, right?" When I saw the look in his eye, I knew that Dr. Trough was very serious. Without even being given the chance to demonstrate my mental skills, I had been rejected from Lakeshore. I had been denied a voice, it seemed, as my future continued to lie in the hands of everyone else but me.

The records later confirmed that I had been "neither accepted nor rejected." That made no sense; how is it possible to be neither accepted nor rejected? Looking about at all the white faces, I began to wonder about their entry criteria.

I learned, over time, that the nebulous decision could not be justified one way or another. I was not treated with dignity, and the interview was conducted in a condescending manner. Momma would not let me get a word in edgewise, and I believe that she may have swayed Dr. Trough from further consideration with her stories of my inability to feed, dress, or clean myself.

When our meeting was finally over, I left Lakeshore explosive, angry, and verbally abusive. The unjustifiable defeat infuriated me. Because I felt so confident I would get in, I had packed all my favorite tapes, belongings, and assistive devices for my therapy and training. I raged at Momma all the way back to Tuscaloosa.

"Why, Momma? How could you do such a thing?"

"Boy, shut yo' mouth! Now you know damn well dat you couldn't do de things dey want you to do. You cain't even put yo'self to bed, Nathan, let alone hold down a job!"

"Momma, you d . . . don't want me to be nuthin' in life, do you?"

"It ain't dat I don't want you to be nuthin', it's jus' dat you cain't be nuthin'."

"Ada, why you keep tellin' Nathan that? Nathan can be any damn thing he wants to be if you would quit tellin' him that he cain't. When I came outta de hospital, a lot of people told me dat I wouldn't be nuthin', but chou see me and Annie got our own house an' our own car. We ain't askin' nobody for a damn thing!"

"You see, brother Nora, you kin use yo' hands; you kin read. Who in dey right mind gonna give someone a job who cain't read?"

I silently made up my mind that I would find a way to prove this woman wrong, no matter how long it took me. I was more determined than ever to make something out of myself. Somehow I had to find a way to learn how to read and write. I needed to prove to her, and more importantly, to myself, that I was as capable as anyone else of being an asset instead of a liability. I began to reassert to the staff at the center my desire to get a high school diploma, this time with an even further-reaching goal. I wanted to go to the

University of Alabama, and Dr. Holder had some thoughts of her own on the subject.

"Do you know what you are asking, Nathan? There will be long, hard hours of intense study. Since you are just beginning to learn the basics, it will be a long time before you are ready to take the GED."

This upset me, because up until that time I had thought I was ready. Down deep I knew I really wasn't, but I didn't want to admit it to myself. I was extremely anxious to meet yet another goal in my life. All this time I had been ignoring the truth, thinking that education was within my grasp, not willing to admit that my disability, my home environment, and the lack of opportunity in my life set me back much further than I originally anticipated. Not that anyone could tell me that.

Beth and I had many heated arguments over the next year. My anger at Lakeshore and Dr. Trough found a vent in the patient, understanding, and encouraging team at the center. I spent a great deal of time confiding in Mary Jo, who sympathized with how I was feeling at the time, but was hesitant in agreeing with my desire to return for yet another try. She encouraged me to pursue the GED, an effort that would require convincing Dr. Holder.

I felt torn between the need to show up one man at Lakeshore and the increasingly enticing prospect of a college career. Doctors like Trough still practice this type of discrimination. Granted, in most cases programs like Lakeshore are not designed for the severely disabled, but how are people like me supposed to have a decent opportunity at employment if we are not given a chance to try? With all the technology developed between then and now, it seems that we should be of more economic advantage than just working on some sort of makeshift assembly line packaging light bulbs, fruitcake, household cleaners, and garbage bags.

When Uncle Nora and I discussed the situation, I tried to tell him that college was next for me. I was looking for some badge of humanity after the inhumane way I'd been recently treated. It makes you feel pretty useless when no one will give you a chance to explore options. Between nudging Dr. Holder toward the GED (an effort proving highly frustrating, and the apparent reason I'd been rejected from Lakeshore), my assumed lack of economic value and my dark pigmentation, I was at my wit's end. Believe me, Uncle Nora set me straight.

"You're not really interested in gettin' an education, are you, Nathan? You are more interested in showin' how damn far you have come in this short time. Life is not a game! You have to take control of your life and make somethin' out of it."

"I'm not takin' anything as a game!"

"When I came out of that damn hospital, I knew it wouldn't be easy, and I had to work extra hard to prove myself again. In order to be somethin' boy, you have to believe that chou are somethin' already."

As I sat there, with tears rolling down my face, I could see his penetrating eyes gazing at me with love. No one had more faith in me than him: "Dat nurse, Miss Naggers, believed in me. Dat same lady took a chance on me. Now it is my time to take a chance on you." Uncle Nora knew the strength of accepting my value purely as a human being, something I wouldn't think about. The worth of an education was actually secondary, and somewhat determined, he was saying, by how I looked at myself.

Beth began to instruct me in basic math, English, science, and social studies. Eventually, through funding arranged and jointly provided by the Tuscaloosa Board of Education and a University of Alabama grant, a GED training program, the first of its kind in the state of Alabama for disabled adults, was established at West Alabama Comprehensive Services. All of this came about as a result of the debates between Beth, Dr. Holder, and me. Our first GED instructor was Nancy Hanks.

I was thrilled to be preparing for my high school diploma. Beth gave me a book of Mother Goose nursery rhymes to practice. The work was very difficult and the characters were white, but for the first time in ages I felt like real progress was being made toward my eventual independence and literacy. Every evening, upon returning home, Uncle Nora would sit with me as I shared what I had learned earlier that day. He could hardly believe the progress I was making.

We worked together on homework assignments. He would coach me along, making sure that I stayed on task. If I didn't quite understand something in class, he or Ray would make it clearer to me at home. My education was a team effort. Whenever Momma asked what Uncle and I were doing, I would just say, "Oh, nuthin', Momma. He's just helpin' me learn how to read." She had no problem with that. Very few of her peers could read at all.

Their encouragement was necessary because I was deeply troubled. The Lakeshore disaster took its toll on my self-esteem. I needed something else, besides my studies and my relationship with God, to give me a sense of personal achievement. Mary Jo insisted that my rights had been violated, and my name was submitted for reconsideration, but I was through with Lakeshore. I was afraid of failure and certain that I would be discriminated against because of my color and impoverished history.

In September of 1976, Beth had given me a copy of *Robinson Crusoe* to begin reading at home and at the center. A difficult task to achieve, I would learn to read and comprehend it. Uncle Nora and I practiced together. He had some basic reading skills and taught me all he knew, sitting out under the cherry tree. Our communication became a shared lesson, as Uncle's abilities improved and mine developed.

If I became discouraged, he would rouse me with his counsel, "Finish the book, Nate. Learnin' to read will open up an entire universe dat you will never take for granted." His interest was inspiration enough for me. I finished the book in two months. Beth allowed me to keep it as a trophy. Finally, at 22 years old, I was literate, and the world took on a different shape.

It's a miracle, really, to read. Signs, billboards, magazines, and a variety of other written words became comprehensible to me, and my biggest thrill was reading the Bible. The story of Sampson and Delilah is one of Uncle Nora's favorites, and I chose that to be my first. Literacy made me free in one more aspect of my personal life. No longer could I be engulfed in the ignorance that had been my early childhood, and reading proved to be an essential tool during my work at the next Camp Challenge, to be held December 27–31 down in Florida.

In early November we received a postcard from Milton, who was stationed in Naples, Italy. I was always thrilled to hear from my brother and about his various exploits in far away places. It was not the same as having him with us, though, and I often wondered what he would look like now, my well-traveled and marine-weathered brother. He sent exciting news, exactly the kind we had all been waiting for: Milton was coming home. Many months had passed since any of us had seen him, and Momma was elated by the news.

He arrived in Birmingham on the Tuesday before Thanksgiving and had to spend that night at the bus station, catching a ride home the following morning. At the center Wednesday, I was a veritable wreck. Unable to concentrate on anything, all I managed to do was get on everyone's nerves. I called home twice but to no avail. Milton did not get into town until that afternoon. I was sitting in the living room watching television when he walked in the door.

He looked fit and kind of funny without a thick head of hair. The fat from his years of football had transformed itself into muscle, away from his waist and into his upper body. He had managed to keep his boyish smile but had a mysterious air about him now. Military life had brought out the serious side in my brother, and I realized as he hugged me that Milton had grown up.

We spent as much time together as his hectic schedule would allow. Milton brought back a stereo for me to keep in trust until he returned. It remains in my possession today. For many years I listened to my favorite tapes and records on it. He was intensely interested in all the changes taking place in my life and the trials I had undergone in his absence. Milton strongly encouraged me to attend the next Camp Challenge.

We went to the movies that Friday, following a magnificent Thanksgiving dinner, during which Milton divulged the location of his next home: Barcelona, a port town on the coast of Spain. He was looking forward to the next six months, during which his new skills would be put to the test. We took Milton to the airport on Sunday afternoon, and he put me in the car himself. I was sad to see him leave, but not worried or upset. I was content in the knowledge that Milton had found his calling in life. I was still searching for mine, and that search would take me back to Florida very soon.

Going Beyond My Limitations

This time around, Camp Challenge was not a wilderness venture. It was chosen as the setting for the preliminary discussion and planning of the National United Cerebral Palsy Convention held annually in the District of Columbia. In addition, delegates were to be chosen who would represent the southeastern district of the United States. Both a disabled and nondisabled party would be elected at the camp. Kenny Vasser, former president of West Alabama UCP, submitted my name as our district representative to the national office in New York.

A letter confirming my appointment was then sent back to Kenny, who in turn gave it to Dr. Holder. She brought it to me, and we began the long, arduous process of readying me for the trip, nearly a month away. Selecting a suitable attendant took top priority. Dr. Holder recommended the services of Tom Davis, one of her undergraduate students majoring in Orthopedic Handicapped and Other Health Impaired (OH/OHI), then known as Multiple Disabilities. I met with him later in the semester, and the two of us hit it off immediately.

Tom Davis was an articulate, witty sophomore who made me laugh with his off-the-wall jokes and stories about campus life. After Christmas with his family in Alexander City, he agreed to meet me at the Tuscaloosa Airport, where together we would fly to Atlanta. From there we would fly via Delta Airlines to Orlando.

I was delighted by the prospect of traveling in an airplane. It was to be my first time ever seeing an airplane up close, and the opportunity to fly gave me something to look forward to.

Mary Jo and I sat for many hours discussing what would be expected of me at the conference. I learned how to behave, what to wear, and how to express myself clearly. Kenny brought me a Concerned Youth for Cerebral Palsy (CYCP) Manual and a UCP Manual. Over Christmas I familiarized myself with the detailed information in both books. Everyone expressed to me the need to discuss issues like the education of handicapped children, teacher certification, development of curriculum for the disabled in public schools, advocacy, and many other concerns of the southeastern district.

Preparations for the actual trip were long and involved. While at the center, Beth outlined safety measures, went over rules and procedures, and raised my level of understanding relating to UCP/CYCP goals and objectives. At home, Uncle Nora and I talked about the importance of teamwork. I learned how the family cared for me, in order to better instruct Tom. Things would go smoothly on our trip.

I had difficulty convincing my friends and family that I hadn't fabricated some crazy story, until Kenny Vasser dropped by the house unexpectedly on Friday, December 22, 1976. As he placed two airplane tickets in my hand, I saw all doubt vanish from the faces of those nonbelievers. A certain sense of pride emanated from Momma's face, and word spread like wildfire through the neighborhood, "Nathan Ballard's goin' to Florida on a' airplane!" When I was wheeled into Shedric Davis's Hair and Style for a haircut that evening, I was greeted by a large group of people.

"Nate, heard dat chou are goin' to Florida on a' airplane."

"Yeah, I am goin' to Florida."

"How long you be gone?"

"'Bout four or five days."

"What chou goin' for?"

"I'm goin' fo . . . for a conference to represent a . . . all of West Alabama, and the southeastern district of United C . . . Cerebral Palsy down there."

"Come over here, boy. I'm gonna give you one of my special haircuts, so you look sharp, and dey gonna know how important you are!"

The customers in his shop repeatedly asked me to tell the story of how this came about. You see, in my old neighborhood, people didn't travel in airplanes much, unless they were in the armed forces. Most folks didn't have reliable cars and took the bus long distances because it was a much cheaper mode of transportation than air travel. By the time my family and I were ready to leave for the Tuscaloosa Airport, everyone I knew had extended their congratulations. I was sitting on top of the world, thanking God for the opportunity.

Christmas Day we had gathered at Aunt Joyce's for the yearly festivities. She had prepared a feast: turkey and dressing, cranberry sauce, congealed salad, cooked yams, ham, cakes, pies, and eggnog spiked by Uncle Nora with a little Johnnie Walker Scotch whisky, unknown to my Aunt, of course. The absence of Milton put a slight damper on the celebration, but we had an excellent time nonetheless. The ceremony gave me a rare opportunity to express the importance of what I was doing and clarify some things with my entire family. For the first time, they were beginning to collectively understand and find value in my efforts to achieve independent living.

My stories inspired them, and Momma was coming around to the reality that I was becoming a man. As usual, she helped me pack for the trip later that night. While we packed, I noticed a change in her. Pride radiated from her face, and I saw her viewing me as I'd seen her look upon my brothers' and sisters' successes.

Most of my family met us at the airport the following afternoon around one-thirty to see me off. Tom appeared, and we checked in our baggage. Before handing over my wheelchair, Uncle Nora pulled me aside for a final word of advice.

"Nathan, you have been blessed with this honor. Take full advantage of it. You are now at a point in your life where you can help a lot of people besides yo'self. Remember, son, be true to yo'self and fight like hell for the cause dat chou goin' for. When I look back and see how far you have come, it makes me so proud of you. There's a lot'a people dat's put a lot'a faith in you now, son, so do the best you can."

I was taken out of my wheelchair and placed in a loading lift-seat. From there, Tom transported me to my chair on the plane. As I was being buckled in, I glanced out the window, and saw my family. How far away they all seemed! Tom, sitting next to me, and the smiling flight attendants reminded me not to be nervous. The plane taxied onto the runway, and I caught a glimpse of the proudest expression on my Uncle's face. Any anxiety I felt was put to rest, as the plane took off and my adventures began.

The Delegate

As our plane landed in Atlanta, my excitement began to build. A wheelchair was waiting for me to use while inside the complex. The two hour layover gave Tom and me ample time to explore the airport. It was gigantic, the biggest structure I had ever seen! We found the Delta concourse and quickly grabbed a couple of hot dogs for dinner. The TV screens everywhere were filled with various programs and unfamiliar numbers. Tom taught me how to read boarding information and departure and arrival times. Everyone else was just bored, checking out local programs on screens in waiting areas, reading something, maybe grabbing a cold beer, while waiting on planes just like we were.

Once we boarded the plane and got ourselves situated, Tom ordered us a couple of mixed drinks, and I must say the flight was very enjoyable. My mind was pretty befuddled by the time we landed in Orlando, around 10:30 p.m., because we partied during the entire flight. The first thing I noticed about Florida was the beauty of the night sky and the warm, humid weather, about seventy-two degrees. Tom helped me into my own wheelchair, waiting for me at the baggage claim. We gathered our belongings, took a short bathroom break, and boarded a bus for Sorrento.

Anticipation of the upcoming events was palpable among all the passengers. There was a buzz of conversation as we got to know one another, introducing ourselves and seeking common ground. These people meant business, and I saw that a great deal could be accomplished here. The future for the cerebral palsy political agenda would be determined in the next few days at this series of public forums, of which I was to play a definitive part.

We arrived at Camp Challenge after midnight and were briefed on the next day's activities as we munched on some prepared sandwiches in the dining hall. Afterward, we gathered up our luggage and headed off to our cottages for a few hours of sleep. Tom and I had fun trying to get me situated in a bunk bed. I fell out of it in the middle of the night, waking everyone in my cottage. The landing was hard and I was sore, but okay. The rest of the night was gracefully uneventful.

After an early wake-up call, showers, and a hearty breakfast, we gathered in the auditorium for our orientation meeting. Independent living, sexuality, education, legislation, and family were just some of the issues we were going to deliberate on. Each of three daily meetings would last approximately two hours, followed by an hour break before the next. I could hardly wait to jump into our first topic that first afternoon, psychological and social impact of the disabled on modern society.

Over the next two days we formulated a referendum which was voted on and approved by the majority of us. It covered some necessary changes in the national attitude. These changes would increase both awareness of the needs of disabled citizens and open a variety of new doors for us. They would also challenge passive discrimination toward persons with disabilities in business, housing, and civic life.

These included addressing politically correct speech concerning labeling the disabled. Also, accessible public and private buildings were not as widespread as today across America, even in some big cities. This needed to be remedied. UCP was to be given the final draft for review.

Afterward, we were told to write down our names for a surprise drawing to win a day at Disney World with Anson Williams, the actor who played Potsie on *Happy Days*. We waited in fierce anticipation as the name was drawn. *Happy Days* had always been one of my favorite shows, and you can imagine my sheer joy when Richard Brooks, one of the conference directors, announced Tom and me as the winners!

Anson officiated as the National Celebrity Honorary Chairperson for UCP in 1976, and I was looking forward to meeting him with much anticipation. Together, Tom and I waited at the front gates of Disney World for the arrival of our famous companion. I didn't know what to expect. It was hard to imagine Anson Williams as anything other than a television star. I didn't want to make a fool out of myself or embarrass him in any way. Tom encouraged me to be myself, and after the initial awe passed that's exactly what I did.

Anson turned out to be a funny and strikingly human guy, much like everyone in Hollywood, I suspect. He pushed me around during most of the afternoon. We had a great time together, riding the various and sundry park contraptions. The most memorable experience of the day proved to be the Wild West roller coaster ride. All of those ups and downs, jerks and jolts in the dark, and dizzy speed proved that ride to be as thrilling as it was terrifying.

The day passed much too quickly. "You are one amazing person, Nathan. I've never met anyone quite like you before," Anson told me as we rode back to camp late that afternoon. After dinner, he addressed the conference, expressing his own observations and hopes for the future. I shall never forget Anson Williams. He taught me that celebrities have the same needs and fears, regardless of their successes or failures, as other people do. I also witnessed the power of his integrity. Presenting myself in the most direct and honest way possible has been an important and difficult lesson throughout my life.

I could not have found this out at a better time. From the six UCP divisions, we were to elect two representatives for the upcoming White House Conference on Handicapped Individuals. All debates and discussion during the Ford administration about public policy pertaining to disabled Americans would come to their fruition in this, the first meeting of its kind called by the federal government in the history of the United States. Without hesitation, I made a decision to run for one of the seats. Here was opportunity to become an even greater voice for the people. As the information for all concerned parties was explained by Jack Smith, the executive director, I whispered over to Tom, "I want this; I want this bad!" He agreed to help me wage an effective campaign.

Together, we brainstormed for a catchy phrase to use and came up with "Salt and Pepper." Tom's idea, which I liked very much, made use of our different skin tones to show our virtual compatibility. On a deeper level, our individual flavors enhanced our ability to spice up the environment we would become involved with. As signs and speeches were made over the next day and a half, Camp Challenge became a political arena. Tom and I fought to get our message across: "Disabled people have the unalienable right to live like everyone else. The world must know that it is everyone's responsibility to defend that right."

Thursday afternoon, in the main auditorium, the votes were cast. Cautiously optimistic, Tom and I were pumped up when we arrived at the banquet that evening. We were certain about the support of a portion of the crowd but not enough to be overly confident. I can't express in words how badly I wanted this appointment, because working on a national level to fulfill my greatest dream, equality, seemed to me to be the culmination of everything my life represents. Dressed in sharp formality, it felt like Oscars night and I was up for Best Actor.

Following dinner, Jack Smith, the executive director of the White House conference, together with the other speakers at the head of the crowd, called us to order. As he prepared to announce the first delegate, I kept saying, "Let it be me! Please God, let it be me." He read out the name of Kathy Pertuit. During the thunderous applause, I told myself, "I gave it my best. If I don't get this, at least I can be sure of that much." Jack hushed the crowd for the revealing of the second name.

"Nathan Ballard, UCP/CYCP of Tuscaloosa and West Alabama," echoed throughout the dining hall. I shrieked aloud in sheer ecstasy, barely able to hear my own voice, while cheers and congratulations engulfed me. I was dreaming until Kathy rushed over and threw her arms around my neck in mutual acknowledgment of what had just transpired.

She and Tom wanted to go out and celebrate, but I could not. With the full realization of this covenant the others had made with me, my new responsibilities and their inherent possibilities were beginning to hit me, and I needed time alone. Tom and Kathy were unable to understand this change in my mood, and I begged them not to take it personally. At my request, Tom wheeled me back to the dormitory, where I was left in the dark to ponder, musing upon the momentous evening.

I thanked God for giving me the gifts to represent Him in the best way I knew how. I reflected on the words of Uncle Nora, his many lessons, sound advice, and what the look on his face would be when I shared all of this with him.

". . . In order to be somebody, Nate, you've got to believe that you are somebody already . . ."

As I sat quietly and gazed out the window, the clear light of a full moon bathed the night sky. I could still hear the commotion continuing in the dining hall, as conferees began to gather out on the pavilion for a farewell dance. I entered into silent prayer and was spiritually overcome.

When Tom and Kathy came to get me, we sat down by the lake to discuss all of this and what it meant to us as friends and colleagues. Afterward, I placed a call to Beth Bruden, who was ecstatic! Momma was equally thrilled when I told her the news, and agreed to keep it a secret. Tom wheeled me into the dance hall, where a rock-and-roll band was playing what I remember was a Crosby, Stills and Nash tune about Vietnam. Mystical wisps of thought tickled my brain all night, as I jammed out with a girl named Peggy.

The next morning, on New Year's Eve, we caught a plane back home following the closing banquet. Our conference had been a notable success, and the path had been laid toward a voice in Washington for disabled youths across the country. Kathy Pertuit and I were to be a part of that voice.

We agreed to correspond with one another weekly, exchanging tapes and comparing notes in preparation for the Washington trip scheduled in April. We were asked to draft a comprehensive report including major goals and objectives covered during Camp Challenge, a thorough evaluation of the conference, and other relevant information. Between GED classes and this, I had my hands full, but nothing could stop me from meeting both obligations. Peter and my friends at the center would play an integral part in contributing information desperately needed for the White House conference. In addition, I had a pending interview with Sally Tucker from the Tuscaloosa News, informing the public of the importance this conference held for people with multiple disabilities. I was eager to get started.

January 17th

I awoke on Monday, January 17, 1977, with a distinct feeling of trepidation. Working diligently toward my GED tests, I had been making considerable progress, but I knew this was not going to be a good day from the very start. My family was tense. That was the first Christmas Milton had ever been away, and his only share in our holiday came in the form of a postcard from Naples, Italy. Momma never really got over Milton joining the marines, and the scandal which arose following his enlistment only made matters worse.

The truth is, Milton was hoodwinked by an unfaithful secret wife! The situation is confusing, but I will try to explain. He had a girlfriend in school who, for legal purposes, we will call Angela. This is their chaotic story.

Milton truly loved Angela, and they shared a physical union during his senior year of high school. Immediately following his departure for basic training, Angela found herself pregnant with another man's child. Her mother, upon discovering Angela's condition, demanded to know if Milton was the father. Angela knew that my brother was not the father of her child, but she knew Milton was a marine and therefore could be held financially responsible for the child's rearing. The real father was a lowlife scumbag, and Angela's mother, though an alcoholic, was very cunning and manipulative.

She concocted a brilliant scheme. Milton was underage and needed a consent form, with Momma's signature, to be married. Now, Milton had a close friend, whom we will call George. George's mother was a drinking buddy of Angela's mother. Are you confused yet? You're not nearly as much as I was!

With George acting as Milton, and George's mother acting as Momma, they faked a marriage and obtained a license! The deal was, the two mothers would use the money they could get to support their drinking habits. When Milton returned home over Thanksgiving for his ten-day leave, Angela and her mother scared Milton into believing there was nothing he could do. Feeling powerless, he was coerced into filling out an allotment form to pay for a child he believed himself to be the rightful father of. George was innocent in the scheme and had acted in what he believed to be the best interests of his friend.

Milton, in good conscience, came home to marry Angela unaware the child was not his or that she had been cheating on him while they where still in school. He discovered himself already married! To make matters worse, the girl's mother threatened Milton with a paternity lawsuit and exposure if he did not comply with her demands. Milton's chief concern was keeping all of this from his own family. He did not want to hurt anyone, especially Momma. He left for Spain with this burden in his heart.

At 2:20 a.m. on the morning of January 17, tragedy struck. In the dense fog of Barcelona Harbor, a three-hundred-eighty ton Spanish freighter, the *Urela*, collided with an ill-fated fifty-six-foot navy landing launch carrying approximately one hundred U.S. Navy seamen and marines back to their respective ships. The Sixth Fleet helicopter carrier, *Guam*, and the amphibious transport U.S.S. *Trenton* were waiting further out in Barcelona Harbor. The impenetrable blanket of fog shielded the oncoming launch from view of the *Urela*, moving dead ahead. As the launch rounded the pier, the resulting collision overturned the launch in a tremendous crash.

We first heard of the accident on the *CBS Morning News*. The number of lives lost was estimated at forty-six, after the initial head count. They were recovering bodies even as the newscast was being given, and no names would be released until all families of the deceased had been notified. I was in shock, and a numb disbelief pervaded my being.

Momma said, "My God, I hope Milton is all right. I hope he's all right." We went through the morning routine in gloomy silence. As Momma got ready for work, I was picked up by a bus from the center. Beth knew that something was wrong with me immediately. I explained the circumstances and continued my GED studies, silently vowing to Milton that come what may, I would get my diploma and go on to college.

That was the longest day of my life. I came home in the afternoon to a bewildering scene. Uncle Nora, Auntie, and Joyce were all sitting around the television waiting for news of any kind. The 5:30 p.m. report revealed the number of men killed from Alabama to be three. As I looked into space, my very soul cried out in anguish. I knew my brother was among them.

This was confirmed by Nick Brown, a Northport policeman and long-time friend of the family. He knocked on the door, and Momma broke into tears, screaming hysterically. He rushed in and took hold of her.

"Three men will be coming by soon to talk with you."

"What about . . ."

"Ada, I have no idea."

"My son . . . he's dead, isn't he Nick?"

"I don't know."

"You know dat Milton is dead, don't chou Nick?"

"I can't give you any more information than that. I'm sorry, but that's all I can tell you. I'm sorry."

They came about fifteen minutes later, a chaplain, Captain Smith, and another officer, revealing Milton to be among the first recovered casualties. Milton was one of the servicemen closest to that section of the launch which received the catastrophic blow. Trapped at the point of impact, Milton's neck broke, killing him instantly, as the launch split in half. Captain Smith informed us that Milton's body would be shipped to Wilmington,

Delaware. From there, a special plane would fly him home. A marine would remain with the body until the time of burial. After expressing their heartfelt sympathy, the three men respectfully departed.

An official military confirmation of his death came in a telegram from General Louis H. Wilson, Commandant of the United States Marine Corps. Governor George Wallace and President Gerald Ford also sent their condolences. My brother was dead, and that's all that mattered to me. No one in my house slept that night. The fact that I would never see him again was difficult enough to deal with, but the situation quickly became considerably stickier.

The next morning, Angela and her mother came over, demanding that the body, funeral arrangements, and all personal affects of Milton's be turned over to them immediately. The look of unbelieving horror on my mother's face still chills me to this day, as she saw the marriage license in Angela's seventeen-year-old hand. The girl had a frenzied look on her stupid face, as she leapt around screaming, "My husband is dead, and the money is mine! All . . . MINE!!!!" They were referring to the twenty-thousand-dollar insurance money from the government, which now would go to them.

This blatantly inhumane action maddened me to the point of violence. Fuming inside, I said nothing. All I wanted to do was grieve in peace. The family relinquished nothing, believing her to be a liar. The resulting skirmish out on the front lawn, between my sisters and them, landed Angela and her mother out on their butts in the street. Angela's mother left with her daughter yelling something about how Milton was hers now, dead or alive.

By the end of the week, most of Milton's belongings, including the car, were in the hands of Angela and company, who proceeded to wreck the car the following week, before the funeral had even taken place. Momma waged an enthusiastic but fruitless campaign to try to get what rightfully belonged to her. The money was given to Angela about a month later, and she moved to Michigan the following year. Her mother died in 1991 of cirrhosis and cancer. Her son, last I heard, attended the University of Michigan, unaware that the name he carries, Ballard, is not his in truth.

I have not seen him since Angela left Northport, and I hold no animosity toward him, nor do I wish to cause him pain. But the truth, God help us, is the truth. Angela is somewhere in Michigan, though I know not where. Momma's mental state has been severely strained, for obvious reasons. Her nerves forced her into an early retirement one year later. I included this story in my book to clear my brother's name from any further misconceptions. Now, with a long-open wound closed, may he finally rest in peace.

The funeral service was long and involved. After a moving sermon, everyone headed to Cedar Oak Cemetery, where a twenty-one gun salute was fired and taps was played as he was lowered into the ground. Lance Corporal Milton Ballard, you left this world for a better place. Your example has taught me to value each day of my life as unique and infinitely precious. I will always love you and look forward to being with you again, up above.

Running the Race

During the weeks following Milton's death I became more determined to make my dream of going to the University of Alabama a reality. It was the last promise I made my brother, and I would get my GED, come hell or high water. The pace was irritatingly slow, and I worked rigorously as Beth drilled me in English, math, social sciences, and history. We had the specially hired instructor, but Beth had seen my determination and put forth an extra effort on my behalf. She took additional time out of her day, around lunch time, to work with me on a one-on-one basis.

She also sought to prepare me for my upcoming duties in Washington. The Rehabilitation Act of 1973, the pioneering disabled rights bill, would soon be passed into law. The bill was drafted in 1973 but wasn't passed until 1978 because of the tremendous debate that ensued. The upcoming conference would address issues relating to its passage and the subsequent effect it would have on the country. Beth set up a meeting for me with Dr. David Mathews, who had just resumed his position as president of the University of Alabama.

While serving an appointment as Secretary of Health, Education and Welfare from 1976 to 1977, Dr. Mathews pushed legislation he had been developing for years with a team deliberating and experimenting in Washington and Tuscaloosa. The act, which became known in law as Section 504, provides for equal opportunity of the disabled to receive federal grants and programs, eliminating discrimination in education, the work place, housing, and a wide spectrum of other areas. It contains allotments for remedies and attorney fees should any disabled individual feel his or her rights have been violated. Section 504 was the first of its kind, causing a great deal of controversy nationwide. No one knew the bill better than its author, and Beth wanted to give me the chance to meet him. If I was ever to attend classes at the University of Alabama, it would be with the help of this man.

Dr. Mathews is one of the most kindhearted men in the entire world. Champion of the disabled, author, and personal friend, Dr. Mathews made possible the fulfillment of another dream of mine. Our conversation was basically dominated by my intense interest in attending classes at the University of Alabama. He suggested that I apply for New College, a program which allows a cross section of students with unique needs to develop an individualized major using all the resources of the university.

We struck up a deal. If I would finish all GED tests within a year, Dr. Mathews would see how soon I could be interviewed for possible admission into New College. To check up on my progress, he would periodically send Donna Milligan, his assistant, over to the center. With that discussion out of the way, I was able to concentrate on the issues we were raising in Washington.

Dr. Mathews was very interested in this conference. The bill eventually gained overwhelming support, and its passage was all but assured. This conference was designed to discuss the best ways of implementing the new laws, and their subsequent effect on the nation. Job and housing discrimination would be much more difficult than in the past. No federally funded program could easily discriminate against the disabled. Additionally, all public buildings and transportation were required by law to create accessibility for the disabled, including parking. All who complied with the regulations within a three to five year period would receive a significant tax break.

In addition, each state would be required to establish a developmental disabilities planning council. This was designed to address issues on a more personal level, so individuals with disabilities would have a voice on their own behalf, should any lack of compliance with the new law become evident. Violations of personal rights or dignity could be challenged in court, on a state level, by lawyers working for each federally funded program on behalf of any individual with a disability. Governor Wallace had designated the Law School of the University of Alabama to house a national pilot program in 1976. Thus, Alabama Disabilities Advocacy Program (ADAP) was born.

I left Dr. Mathews's office with a deeper understanding of the task before me. I came home that afternoon, exhausted by the day's activities. Nora saw a look of frustration on my face, and suggested we sit under our favorite cherry tree for a little chat.

"Nate, I can tell that chou ain't yo'self. What's de matter wit' chou?"

"Uncle, I feel very tired, and don't know what to do. The GED work is hard, but I got to do dis."

"It's a lot more den dat. Nate, it's dis Washington thing, ain't it?"

"Yeah, how you know that's what it was?"

"You see, son, I been down that road many times. You got doubts, maybe. Doubts dat chou ain't good enough to represent these people. But chou got to understand, dis is the chance of a lifetime! You been workin' through de mail and by phone for about three months wit' dis here girl, and she's got confidence in you. All you need now, is to believe in yo'self a little more."

"But you just don't get it, do you, Uncle? It's not that, not at all."

"You goin' up dere wit' all'a dem educated folks, and you ain't got no formal education yet. Look at the impact of Nat Turner's revolt. How about the words of Malcom X, 'specially past his return from Mecca? Look at President Lincoln. He did not have no kind of formal education, and where did he end up? Lincoln wasn't recognized for anything mo' special than being a man of integrity. The same is true of our peanut-farming president, Jimmy Carter. What about dat man dey call Einstein? He flunked out of high school, and he's a great man too.

"Great men want simply to admit what's broke, and then fix it as easy as possible. I think it's you who don't get it, because Nate, you see, learnin' is a continual process, and don't chou ever believe dat goin' to college is the only way dat chou can learn. It ain't. Use dat God-given talent, uniquely your own."

"What is dat talent, Uncle Nora?"

"Speech, my boy! Your education will only refine the talent already in you. As much trouble as you have speaking, what comes out is almost a poetry in and of itself. You have a bright future ahead of you, son. God knew dis when he gave you dat talent, and I know it too; so do you. We have two choices in life, speak or be spoken for. You will speak in Washington, D.C., for those who are unable to speak for themselves. You have already gone further than any of yo' brothers and sisters, and for that matter, any Jacksons or Ballards in history, to my knowledge. How many people do you think would be in yo' shoes right now?"

As he continued to speak, I began to stare off in the distance. My future was laid out before me, and I silently reaffirmed a commitment to myself. Three days later, Jack Smith sent a formal invitation for me to serve as an elected Delegate-at-Large for the White House conferences. I had ten days before the preparatory seminars and had to find a traveling companion rather quickly.

Kenny Vasser, President of the local UCP chapter, was assigned to be my attendant. Two days before my departure, Kenny came by the center to inform me of a sudden family emergency which had just surfaced. He would be unable to accompany me to Washington.

Under the circumstances, Dr. Holder suggested Melissa McCardney as a suitable replacement. Melissa, a student teacher at the center, was only too willing to go. She had never been out of Alabama in her young life. She is a true southern belle in manners and beauty. Yet for all her gentility, she had a quick wit and the insight of a bright and eager college senior majoring in special education.

Together, we left for Washington, D.C., on Wednesday, April 20, 1977. Uncle Nora and the family, Mary Jo, and Beth saw me off. This day marked the beginning of my career as an advocate for the disabled. The nation's capitol appeared majestic as we passed by the Pentagon and Capitol building from the air. The sun shone down on the Mall from above the intermittent clouds and danced off the national monuments we passed over. Dulles International Airport awaited our arrival below.

"Oh, my God!" Melissa gasped when she saw the sleek black limousine waiting to whisk us away to our hotel. We ran into some trouble in the lobby of the Washington Hilton, because the hotel manager expected Kenny Vassar to be my attendant. The manager called all up and down the East Coast before confirming the validity of her presence. It was one-thirty in the morning before arrangements could be made for Melissa to have a room of her own. Another thirty minutes passed before an attendant arrived who could ready me for bed. Three health personnel were assigned who would tend to my needs for the length of my stay in Washington.

We started with a 6:00 a.m. breakfast and were kept busy until late that evening. The delegation was briefed on the inner workings of this landmark White House conference to be held in the following month of May. I presented a long list of questions relating to conference dynamics and protocol. Kathy and I discovered there was a great deal at stake here.

Advocacy was the main issue: How can we better represent ourselves and the undeniable rights of the disabled needing to be honored and respected by all of America? Each morning at six we were to meet with our Concerned Youth for Cerebral Palsy chairpeople, Doug Shields and Ann Sue Goldberg, to discuss the best plan of attack. We would be heard and our ideas would be considered.

Kathy and I would do our part to challenge elitism and generate a greater climate of understanding and acceptance. We were determined to reduce the tendency toward negative stereotyping, harmful prejudice, and discrimination. As the orientation conference progressed, I was delighted to see everyone striving toward common goals. Melissa's beauty and enchanting wit made even the more serious moments appear less stressful. Although she had never worked with me away from the center, our professional relationship was completely symbiotic.

We participated in workshops all the next morning at our hotel and were also scheduled to meet privately with President Carter at the White House in the late afternoon. A cocktail party at the Russell Senate Building would wind up the evening. We had difficulty getting clearance for Melissa again. The wait was only minutes this time around. Once inside the gates, the Secret Service approached our van.

"We are ordered to inform you . . . the President will be unable to attend your scheduled meeting, due to the Iranian Crisis. His representative from the Office of Public Liaison, Midge Costanza, will be with you momentarily."

Our delegation awaited Ms. Costanza's arrival in an office located at the basement level of the White House. Anticipation reached a fierce level. When she entered the room, questions flew like wildfire:

"Where does President Carter stand on Section 504?"

"The President stands firmly in the defense of the rights of disabled citizens."

"Who would implement Section 504?"

"Each state will have its own advocacy program."

"In what time frame will this become reality?"

"Ideally? Within five years."

Our meeting lasted about two and a half hours. When our van left the White House grounds, each and every one of us felt like we were part of a triumphant historical event. I had little time before the pending cocktail party and went to my room to get ready. Melissa and Kathy met me in the lobby dressed to kill. Together, we left for the Russell Senate Building. A host of Senators and other dignitaries greeted us inside. We began with a

Meet the Press–style question and answer session, followed by a pleasant party with various hors d'oeuvres and mixed drinks. I certainly enjoyed myself immensely.

The next day, Melissa and I snuck in a little sightseeing. I was awestruck by the artwork in the Capitol's Rotunda. Staring up at the Brumidi's *Apothesis of Washington*, in the style of Michaelangelo's frescoes on the ceiling of the Sistine Chapel, in all of its magnificence, I felt like a little child in a toy store for the first time. The many museums, buildings, monuments, and information on the Mall would take even the most able-bodied person a month of nothing but sightseeing to absorb any detail. The sheer beauty of Washington, from the tremendous structures to the blossoming flowers in Capitol Park, made me feel glad to be alive and a free American.

The Zenith

Upon returning, I was greeted by a host of friends offering their congratulations, but the most memorable thing of all was the satisfied look on Uncle Nora's face. It was like a present to me. Everything he had taught me in the past was beginning to coalesce. I was on my road to fulfillment.

Dr. Mathews called for a meeting between us. I gave him information about current legislation and activities in Washington. He introduced me to the Assistant Vice President of the University, Dr. Sutton. After explaining my unique situation to him and sharing with him my desire to take classes, Dr. Sutton asked me a few questions of his own.

"Why do you want to become a student at the university?"

"To better myself."

"Do you have a major in mind?"

"Yes, I sure do! I want to study psychology."

"You do know what it will entail?"

"What do the word entail mean?"

He looked at Dr. Mathews with sudden surprise in his eyes. I don't think he expected me to be so boldly inquisitive, but then again, who does?

"The word entail, Nathan, means what will be expected of you in the course of studying psychology. You are a very intelligent young man."

I took this as a great compliment, coming from a man of such academic standing. Dr. Mathews arranged for me to take sample tests of various parts of the GED, and he warned me to be very astute when taking these mock tests. They would follow a format similar to the real thing. This would all take place following the Washington conference. I could barely contain my excitement.

The next three weeks passed quickly as I intensified my GED studies while simultaneously preparing for my return trip to the nation's capitol. Mary Jo Deaver and I worked together on a speech Jack Smith asked me to give at the actual conference. Rick Roden, my assigned attendant, was also a special education student, majoring in emotional conflict and learning disabilities. Rick was in ROTC and had a vibrant personality. We arrived at Washington National Airport in the early afternoon of May 23, 1977, and boarded a special bus which took us directly to the Sheraton-Park Hotel.

Once registered at the state of Alabama table, we were given a comprehensive registration packet, itinerary, and other conference-related material. The activities were to begin later in the evening at a general assembly in the Grand Ballroom of the Sheraton-Park Hotel. Rick and I took the time to find Kathy. We relaxed for a few hours, grabbed some drinks in the hotel lounge, and went over my speech to be given the following morning.

I was flabbergasted by the immensity and grandeur of the ballroom. President Jimmy Carter delivered a stirring opening address before thirty-two hundred delegates and about nine hundred other guests, the largest national gathering in history for the disabled political agenda. His optimistic tone convinced me that our bill's passage was indeed assured. We were then entertained by a gaggle of musicians, dancers, actors, and other disabled performers before the evening's activities came to a close.

The next morning, we rose early and had breakfast at a local coffee shop right around the corner from the hotel. As Rick and Kathy took turns pushing my chair, I looked around at the stillness of the morning, smelling the fresh flowers. The dew glistened on freshly cut grass below me. It felt good to be back in Washington. The city is only as inspiring as the hopes it represents for your dreams, vision, and comprehensive grasp of America's actual possibilities.

We discussed stage fright at breakfast. I did not want to appear nervous, but sometimes my body acts of its own accord. Even talk on such a subject is enough to cause me unwanted problems. The more I thought about going out on stage in front of so many strangers, the more tense and agitated I became. I couldn't stop my right arm from lashing out and knocking over a glass of freshly squeezed orange juice. Luckily, it merely spilled on the table, mercifully avoiding everyone's clothing.

Then it dawned on me. I was about to voice my thoughts on the most important subject in my life to date. Senators, congressmen, delegates, reporters, and several others were going to listen this morning, as I shared exactly what I thought about having cerebral palsy. I pondered on my experience at Lakeshore and vowed not to let anything silence me this time, least of all the very thing I was about to discuss! I could not let it ruin the chance to share my intimate feelings with the very people who could change things for the better. This was my chance to sway opinions, lobby and influence public servants, or maybe more.

Maybe this was a chance at something most people I knew at the time, and know today, never even think about. Maybe this was a rare chance at citizenship. I mean, I learned studying civics for the GED that American citizenship was, "We the People," deciding on our own laws, governing ourselves, writing and helping shape the policies which govern our lives. Dr. Mathews and I talked for some time about the power of citizenship. Here was the big C-word staring me down, undeniably.

"You okay, Mr. Ballard? Get any orange juice on you?"

"No . . . I'm fine. Great in fact! Uh, sorry about the mess."

With the gravity of this moment in my grasp, I asked God to guide me in this speech, and to give me the grace and courage to triumph in helping the Senate understand why they were voting for the bill. I finished my breakfast with renewed confidence.

We went straight to the Sheraton Ballroom. When it came time for me to speak, Kathy gave me a tremendous hug and whispered encouragement in my ear. As Rick locked my wheelchair in place, I slowly reached between my legs and grabbed the notes I had stuffed there. As I placed them on the podium, a hush fell over the crowd. I paused, took several deep breaths, cracked an awkward grin that caused numerous muffled giggles, and began to speak. At first my voice stammered, but I quickly regained composure:

> Don't believe what your eyes are telling you.
> All they show is limitation.
> Look with your understanding.
> Find out what you already know.
> And you'll see the way to fly.

"That is an excerpt from *Jonathan Livingston Seagull*, a book written by Richard Bach," I said, looking over the crowd. A distinct feeling of calm swept over my being as I explained:

> We don't want your pity or your sympathy. We want your understanding of us as human beings . . . with limitations, but who can achieve through your understanding, thus your help, in all areas. We want to fly, as high as our potentials will allow. We want to know what it's like to earn a wage, to have adequate health care, to be trained to do whatever tasks we may. We have a right to life. Accept us as brothers.

I paused for a moment and looked over the crowd. In the faces of everyone, there existed some kind of emotion. Several people had tears in their eyes, many were smiling, and some were pondering my sentiments, but all were affected. With this in mind, I continued:

> Thou art my brother because you are a human, and we are sons of one Holy Spirit. We are equal and made of the same earth. You are here as my companion along the path of life and my aid in understanding the meaning of hidden truth. You are human; and that fact sufficing, I love you as a brother.
>
> You may speak of us as you choose, for tomorrow shall take you away and will use your talk as evidence for His judgment, and you shall receive justice. You may deprive me of whatever I possess, for my greed instigated the amassing of wealth, and you are entitled to my lot if it will satisfy you.
>
> You may do unto me whatever you wish, but you shall not be able to touch my Truth. You may shed my blood and burn my body, but you cannot kill or hurt my Spirit. You may tie my hands with chains and feet with shackles and put me in the dark prison, but you shall not enslave my thinking for it is free, like the breeze in the spacious sky.
>
> You are my brother and I love you. I love worshipping in your church, kneeling in your temple, and praying in your mosque. You and I are all children of one religion, for the varied paths of worship are but fingers on the moving hand of the Supreme Being, extended to all, offering completeness of spirit to all, anxious to receive all.
>
> I love you for your Truth derived from knowledge; that Truth which I cannot see because of my own ignorance. But I respect it as a divine thing, for it is a deed of the Spirit. Your Truth shall meet my own in the coming world and blend together like the

> fragrance of flowers, to become one whole and eternal Truth, perpetuating and living in the eternity of Love and Beauty.
>
> I love you because you are weak before the strong oppressor, and poor before the greedy rich. For these reasons I shed tears and comfort you; and from behind my tears I see you embraced in the arms of Justice, smiling and forgiving your persecutors. You are my brother and I love you.

As sporadic applause and spontaneous emotional outbursts began, I fought to maintain the attention of the audience for my closing remarks:

> It is my fervent hope that my whole life on this earth will ever be tears and laughter. Tears purify my heart and reveal to me the secrets of life and its mystery. Laughter brings me closer to my fellow men. Tears with which I join the brokenhearted. Laughter symbolizing joy over my very existence.

Thunderous applause and shouts of joy surrounded me! My message had its intended effect, and I knew I had made a difference in the forming opinions of everyone in the auditorium. Kathy and Rick were incredibly proud, and their wholehearted congratulations felt really good. I thanked God repeatedly for His help in carrying out my task. With my input, the potential future for disabled citizens shone like a blinding beacon of light.

Although there were three days left of workshops, voting, and debating, nothing had a greater impact on me than those faces in the crowd as I poured my heart out that morning. Even the Smithsonian museums, of which Kathy, Rick, and I took an afternoon tour, as massively informative as they were, could not compare to the profound change which had come over me. I felt proud to be myself, and free to shout my thoughts and ideals to Heaven itself.

I realized for the first time, regardless of those believing they had cornered the market on who was capable of contributing constructive thought, my ideas and contribution to all ideas were important solely on the basis that they were mine. Even more importantly, in legitimate democracies citizens need to understand each other's needs, rich and poor. Ensuring that the ways and means exist to meet and defend the needs of all our citizens ensures we will remain a collectively mighty and mutually prosperous country. This holds true, I realized, for you, me, and everybody. Before my time on this earth passes, I told God, I will try to share with the whole world the importance of understanding and nurturing this truth.

The Risk

My work with UCP would continue through 1979. I traveled to Chicago, Illinois and Louisville, Kentucky as a Public Affairs Chairman of Concerned Youth for Cerebral Palsy (CYCP), a subcommittee of the national UCP committee. We were in charge of making priorities and recommendations to the national UCP executive board. We had the honor and privilege of traveling to various cities in the nation where our views were considered valuable, and UCP would always foot the bill. CYCP was disbanded in 1981 due to lack of funding, but the work we accomplished has had significant ramifications.

The telethon style of fund-raising changed profoundly with our input. Utilizing the skills of articulate and visibly intelligent young people with cerebral palsy to raise money for the national UCP organization was previously unheard of. We demanded that disabled children no longer be paraded across a stage to invoke pity in a misdirected effort to solicit funds for the national, state, or regional UCP affiliates. Instead we offered the obvious alternative: invite children and adults with cerebral palsy to showcase their indvidual skills and talents toward the same end. Thanks to CYCP, fundraising began to have a more community oriented approach that presented people with cerebral palsy in a more dignified and appropriate light.

A few days after my return home, Dr. Mathews called me to his office in Rose Administration Building for an update on my educational situation. "Nathan, how are things going? Are you making good progress toward our preliminary tests?"

"I am progressing, but not as fast as I want to, Dr. Mathews."

"This is to be expected."

"I want this bad, Dr. Mathews, I want it so bad 'til I can taste it!"

"In order for you to do this, you've got to really make it happen for you and no one else but you."

Over the next few weeks, I pushed myself to the limits of my physical and emotional endurance. Dr. Mathews made special arrangements for me to take a mock social studies test in the GED format at a testing center in the basement of Rose Administration Building. Since I did not have the fine motor skills to fill in answer bubbles, he also arranged for a proxy to fill them in for me. The test was grueling, but I passed it with flying colors!

Dr. Holder and Beth were very surprised. I was amazed, in fact, at just how surprised they seemed, but everyone was behind me now. The looks on their faces only convinced me that Dr. Mathews was right. If this dream was to be realized, it would be through my own perseverance. Every dream I've had took hard work, with my sights set higher as I recognized new opportunities.

Dr. Mathews began to work closely with Dr. Holder because there were certain technical difficulties needing to be addressed. I was still medically labeled as "educable mentally retarded" in order to receive certain benefits. These included transportation to and from and involvement in the program at the Work Activity Center. As such, he was taking a big gamble by allowing me to begin classes at the University of Alabama without my high school diploma. Momma, still my legal guardian even though I was of age, could conceivably sue the university for going against her wishes. We had to move forward with extreme caution.

June of 1976 was a very busy month at the Work Activity Center. We received our third teacher, replacing Beth Bruden, who moved on to become a special education teacher in Birmingham. There, she still resides and has retired after a long and noteworthy career teaching the disabled. Bettye Roberts, Beth's assistant, retired as well.

Our new teacher, Earnestine Calhoun Giles, was a young black woman, the first black teacher on staff in the center's history. An extremely sensitive person with enough wisdom for someone twice her age, Earnie brought an air of academia to the center. She wanted us to have the ability to read, write, and speak more effectively and eloquently.

Up until this point, standard educational curriculum had been on the back burner. We had placed more emphasis on independent living and self-help skills. Now reading and writing would extend beyond inscribing our names and learning our ABCs. We read some books while Beth was there, but the format was passive, similar to bedtime stories; practicum students would come in periodically and read classics like *Treasure Island* and *Huckleberry Finn* to the class. We had little say in what was read to us.

As our enrollment increased, it became necessary to divide our ranks. Each Individual Educational Plan (IEP) was geared toward making us as independent as possible, based on our unique abilities. For example, Peter and I had more formal education than most and were inclined to focus our energies on a level of material too advanced, as of yet, for others in the class. Those who received little or no education prior to their entry into the program were concentrating on basic survival techniques, comparable to my first years at the center.

When Earnie came, she brought with her many innovative ideas. The newer members of our class continued to be read classic literature by practicum students. Peter, Snow, and a few others, myself included, began a more intense program of study. Peter and I had the hardest time with our new material, as we were both preparing to take the GED test. Even today, nothing scares me more than math. Earnie increased the amount of math study in our daily routines. I knew the time was coming when my math skills would be tested for the GED and I dreaded it.

In addition, Earnestine assigned a practicum student to each of us. Every day, on a one-on-one basis, we would practice reading aloud. My first in-class book was *King Arthur*. Reading aloud was no problem for me. I had been doing it at home with Uncle Nora and Milton for years. I found *King Arthur* to be fascinating. I had trouble putting it down, even to eat lunch. To this very day, I will occasionally ride up to the public library and peruse it for a little walk down memory lane.

Our first introduction to professional counseling came in the form of a new staff member at the center named Bill Brewer. Dr. Holder felt a need for someone who could help us deal with the special pressures involved in learning how to manage with our disabilities. Bill also served as a much needed facilitator during student conflicts. He held sessions with family members of students, to minimize unnecessary tension between groups ultimately working in our best interests. Bill was especially useful to me. Although we were only acquainted for a few months before he left, Bill was the first of three psychologists to remove the label of "educable mentally retarded" from my case file.

Section 504 and Public Law 94-142 enabled those with developmental disabilities, like cerebral palsy, muscular dystrophy, and a host of other conditions, to receive federal funding and assistance. Although much progress has been made, including recent legislation in Alabama to include head injury victims under Americans with Disabilities Act (ADA) provisions, there are still some disabling conditions not covered under modern provisions, and the mental retardation stigma extends in unspeakable ways today. There are countless minority children and disabled people who can think, feel, reason, and articulate as well as anyone else, yet are placed under this burdensome label, even in 2000!

Does anyone in Washington care that many competent citizens are being labeled in this way? Most politicians don't even realize the gravity of this problem, or they are unconcerned, never having been put in our shoes. It is much easier and convenient to pat our heads, butter us up, and then send us on our merry little ways with an earful of euphemisms, while the average lawmaker goes home for a good night's sleep, forgetting all about us in the morning. My work in Montgomery has shown me that it is much easier to pass the buck than to stand up and take action with guts and determination, holding each other honestly accountable for jointly made decisions. Maybe we will get power away from powerful lobbyists someday, so major issues that are lacking a cash flow behind them get better and more thorough consideration in the modern political arena.

Both Peter and I were labeled educatable mentally retarded. Our desire to take the GED made such a label an impediment to our progress. You can't get a fair shot at a high school diploma when you're labeled in the first grade as retarded, much less go to college. We didn't realize the can of worms that opened when Peter and I started pursuing our education further, and man, what a pain in the ass it was! Peter asked me one day, "Do you know what we are doing, Nathan?"

"No. Isn't it fun, though?"

"We have come a long way since those early days when Jane was here. Did you expect this so soon? I know I didn't."

"No, I didn't, but I knew we both had enough determination to get here. There's no way some stupid label is gonna keep us from getting any further."

"You fool, what do you want with a college degree anyway?"

"I have a few things in mind. The real question should be why's a crip like you want an education?"

"I thought being president of the United States would be nice for starters, what about you?"

"I'll be a psychologist someday, so I can check your brain, Mr. President!"

Never let it be said that even concerning the most serious subjects, Peter Moore could be anything but lighthearted. His muscular dystrophy was getting progressively worse. The muscular development he worked so hard to maintain was deteriorating at a more rapid rate than any of us realized, including Peter himself. He was a fierce fighter, though, and inspirational to all our efforts. Peter was working on his greatest composition, *The WACS Crest*, to be used in conjunction with the official change in the name of the Adult Work Activity Center to West Alabama Comprehensive Services. Although the two terms are interchangeable, the new name had special significance because it marked a new beginning in our history as a service center. The Adult Work Activity Center became WACS, for short, in August of 1977. Mark Singer, our new resident counselor, climbed up a ladder and nailed a sign bearing the new name to the very top of our building. We had spent two months making that sign during art class, and everyone shouted for joy at the sight of it emblazoned on our house in all of its handcrafted glory. It served as another reminder of our future independence.

Dilemma

From April of 1976 to July of 1977, I struggled to learn four years' worth of high school education, reaching the point of almost giving up. Never again, even in writing this book, have I experienced the type of intellectual exhaustion that plagued my life in those days. I would come home from the center so tired that Momma used to pester me about what was going on at "dat school." I was forced to reveal the secret Uncle Nora and I had kept from her for over a year, and she was furious with me for keeping her in the dark about the GED all that time. When the day of reckoning arrived, Uncle Nora was quick to defend me from her opposition.

"You are doin' something dat's gonna hurt chou in the long run."

"But Momma, this is my way of bettering myself. How can it hurt me at all?"

"He's right you know, dis is gonna help him, and help all of us in de long run. Do you know dat Nate has just got back from Washington? Nate's doin' work with United Cerebral Palsy on both a local and national level. He's doin' bigger an' better things than anyone else in dis family. How long is you gonna keep that attitude you got about dis here boy, Ada?"

"All'a dat may be true, and for dat, I'm as proud of him as you are, but Nora, he's handicapped!"

"Big God-damned deal! You got the closest mind I ever saw in all my years. Dis is yo' boy, Ada! He's sittin' here tryin' to make you proud, an' all you kin do, is knock him down."

"Momma, I am goin' to git my education because I promised Milton dat I would. I don't give a damn whether you like it or not!"

Momma eventually grew to understand my steadfast tenacity, and after years of talking together, Momma has accepted my autonomy. I took the social studies test in September, and passed effortlessly. The science section was next, in November, and it proved to be much more challenging. It took me about four hours to complete and I passed by the skin of my teeth. Peter, however, was surpassing me by leaps and bounds, taking his English, science, and math tests with relative ease. Our childhood rivalry resurged with a vengeance. The whole GED thing was my idea to begin with, and though he was given a motorized wheelchair first, there was no way Peter was going to college before me!

"Nate, Nate, don't you hate, that I'm so fast, and you're so late?"

"I may be late, but I'll run this race, and shove my diploma right up in your face!"

I had a few tricks up my sleeve. While Peter completed the requirements for his GED, I was busily arranging to take a trial class at the university in psychology. Peter was clueless, and I couldn't wait to see the look on his face when he found out what I had been up to behind his back. I was still sore at him for figuring out a way to get a motorized wheelchair before me. In August of 1977, Peter received his new chair from Rehabilitation Services, thanks to Mary Williams, our favorite caseworker. I would not be defeated by him again!

Simultaneously, I had been preparing for and taking various parts of my GED test, while coordinating the details involved in starting class at the university. Dr. Mathews worked, as always, diligently on my behalf.

He introduced me to a delightful lady named Rose Gladney, who was a professor in New College. She explained to me that enrollment is limited to a maximum of two hundred students per semester, who have to enroll before they have completed too many hours of study. New College at the University of Alabama was founded in the Fall of 1971. Rose Gladney and I discussed all of this, and she asked me if I would be interested in enrolling on a trial basis, following my completion of the requirements for the GED test. Would I? She must have been kidding.

"Are you tellin' me that I can become a student?"

"Yes, that is exactly what I am offering you."

"This is a dream come true, Ms. Gladney."

"I know. Dr. Mathews has spoken very highly of you, Nathan. It's a pleasure to finally meet you face-to-face."

"Likewise, believe me!"

"Nathan, what are your ambitions?"

"Well, Ms. Gladney, I would like to write a book about my life."

"With an education, Nathan, that may well be possible."

"May I ask you a question?"

"Certainly."

"Ms. Gladney, is it true that I will be able to start classes in the spring?"

"Maybe so. Dr. Mathews is working out the details. You'll have to talk with him about that."

I continued in my studies and passed the English section in December. After hearing about my success, Dr. Mathews phoned me at WACS with news of his own. The Office of Admissions, at his recommendation, allowed me to enter the University of Alabama System, as a trial student in Psychology 101 for spring semester of 1978. I almost deafened him with my scream of delight. The only condition was that I had to complete the final section of the GED test. Knowing full well what a nightmare mathematics was for me, but determined not to disappoint Dr. Mathews or myself, I agreed to his stipulation. Peter Moore was in for a big shock!

"Earnestine, Earnestine! Come here quick! Hurry!"

"Nathan, are you hurt?"

"No! I have some good news to tell you . . . WHOOWHEE!"

"Calm down, Nathan. Now, tell me what is going on?"

"That was Dr. Mathews on the phone. I will be going to college next semester, Earnie. Here comes Peter! SHHH!"

"What!"

"Earnestine, please! I said, I'll be starting college in the spring."

"Did I just hear Nate tell you he's goin' to college? Yeah right. You just lyin'! Boy, you is lyin' your head off! You ain't startin' no college, not before me!"

At that point, the phone rang. It was Dr. Holder, who called to tell Earnestine what I already had. Peter was so mad, yet he couldn't stop smiling, knowing I had gotten him good. I needed his help now, and he knew it. The only way I was going to pass that infernal math test would be with his assistance.

Peter already had his GED by December, but he had not begun the process of enrolling at the university. Earnestine hung up the phone and told us Dr. Holder was coming by in the afternoon to talk. She had many valid concerns needing to be voiced at this point. I had a pretty good idea what they were.

"Boys, you have to be better than the rest."

"How do you mean, Dr. Holder?"

"I mean you have to be better in this respect. When people look at you now, all they see are two black kids in wheelchairs. You can think, perform, and succeed just as well as they can. In fact, you have got a much greater chance of being successful and finding happiness in your lives than they do. You have had to overcome remarkable odds. Dealing with the question of what to pursue in your college careers will be minuscule by comparison. You two have beaten the odds already!"

I began to smile wider and toothier than ever. I was overflowing with joy, because I knew she was right. As I privately revisited the road of my life, it filled me with pride. I glanced over at Peter and saw a look on his face that left an indelible impression on me. He was thinking along the same lines. We already had so much to feel triumphant about.

"Now, there is another matter at hand. Nathan Ballard, you made all these plans to go to college, and by God, you're in college. There's just one little detail you seem to have forgotten about. How on earth did you intend to get to class? What about getting back? Have you even thought about it?"

"I was aware of this little glitch, but don't worry, Doc. I've thought about it off and on, and it'll work out. Trust me. Everything is under control."

Grinning characteristically, I really had no idea what to do. I always thought Dr. Holder or Dr. Mathews would figure a way around the fact that someone had to push me everywhere I went. I always assumed it would be a practicum student of Dr. Holder's. Right then, I could care less about such trivial details as modes of transportation. The folks at home were in for the biggest surprise of their lives. No one knew I was trying to find a way into college but me and Uncle Nora. Now that I had a foot in the door, it was time to tell Momma.

"Nathan, what is wrong with you, boy?"

"Momma, I have some news dat chou ain't gonna believe!"

"And what might that be?"

"Momma, I am going to be enrolled in a class at the university starting in January."

"Come on Nathan, stop all of that foolish talk. You cain't even write chour name, an' you goin' to college?"

"Momma, call the school and talk to Earnestine. I believe you'll find there's a lot of things I can do you don't even know about!"

"Ada, Annie an' me just got a call from Nate's school."

"Nora, Nathan tells me some nonsense about he goin' to college in January."

"Ada, it's not no nonsense. Nate is goin' to college. I'm very proud of you, son."

I Went the Distance

I think of myself as someone who can be a great deal of help with sorting through other people's problems and getting them back on the right track. Psychology 101 had an interesting course description. Besides, it is the prerequisite for all other psychology courses. Special education would perhaps be my minor. I wanted to understand every detail involved in any disabled educational field, such an extensive part of my life.

Johnny Nash, the driver for WACS, brought me over to Gordon Palmer Hall, where my first class was scheduled to meet. I could hardly believe it! My college career was about to begin! He wheeled me into a lecture hall where students were gathering. Dr. Jerry Rosenberg was the class instructor, but the man who stepped up in front of the class introduced himself as Dr. Michael Roberts. Realizing something was amiss, I raised my hand, and got his attention. "Dr. Roberts . . . I think I'm in the wrong class."

"What is your name, young man?"

"Nathan Ballard."

"Where are you supposed to be?"

I asked him to call Dr. Mathews's office and . . . uh . . . find out. I sat through the first lecture for Developmental Psychology because he wanted to wait until after class to contact Dr. Mathews. I'm glad he did. The class was profoundly interesting, and I assured him it would not be long until I was ready to take his course. Dr. Roberts and I have become good friends over the last several years. He is now at the University of Florida.

The next day I found my class and met Dr. Rosenberg for the first time. Being the jovial, humorous, and intellectual man that he is, we immediately hit it off. Dr. Rosenberg took a great deal of his spare time going over lecture material with me during the semester. I couldn't have done it without his help. I was delighted to earn a C, and Dr. Mathews was equally pleased. During the semester, on the third try, I even passed the math section of the GED test. I was awarded my coveted certificate on January 12, 1979.

Having a high school diploma is a tremendously good feeling. Most people in today's world take such privileges for granted, but I can't tell you how much it meant to me when I opened that manila envelope from the State of Alabama Department of Education.

"Nate! Nate! I have a letter here for you from de state of Alabama. It's some official-lookin' envelope!"

"Give it here, Uncle Nora! Give it to me now!"

"Come on, boy! Open it! It may be your certificate!"

"Nora, it ain't no certificate. Nathan jus' tellin' a bunch of stories. He ain't got no certificate. Dat boy is jus' talkin' out of his head!"

"Ada, give dat boy some credit now. He has worked his ass off to prove something to you. Leave him be. You are more handicapped than he will ever be!"

With feverishly shaking hands, I tore into the envelope. The sight of my equivalent high school diploma filled me with an indescribable sense of accomplishment. To put this in a better perspective, let me offer this much: In the twenty-year history of the WACS program, only Peter, Snow, and I earned GED certificates.

Pretty sad, isn't it? I'm not sure why. There are some smart cookies in the program. I suspect there are political or financial reasons why Peter and I are the only two to have entered college through WACS to date. The preservation of an institution is no reason to impede individual progress of the severely disabled toward more inclusion in higher education.

The grant providing funding for the WACS program requires a yearly evaluation of each client's situation regarding new equipment to potentially update each IEP. One of the objectives of mine was to eventually be trained in the use of an electric wheelchair. Before Peter received his chair, the use of electric assistive devices was foreign to the program. On my behalf, Earnestine decided to consult Buddy Mason, a physical management consultant and therapist familiar with electric wheelchairs and other orthopedic equipment.

I had met Buddy in 1969 during my involvement with Crippled Children's Services. He was already familiar with my physical capabilities and with what would be required of a wheelchair designed to meet my vehicular needs. I was thrilled to hear Buddy was coming back to visit. Previously I failed his test, but now I had a surprise in store for him.

Earlier, in March of 1978, Buddy had arranged for me to try driving a motorized wheelchair for the first time. The results were simply disastrous!

"Now, Nathan, be careful when you do this. It's a very small room, and I know you are excited. This is what I want you to do: Make a full circle. I want you to pivot the chair 360 degrees. It shouldn't be too difficult for you."

"Okay, here we go." I successfully made the turnaround.

"Very good! Now, carefully pull out into the hallway, and then you will need to . . ."

CRASH!!

In my haste, I had pushed the joystick forward too far, and bulleted my footplate through the hollow door to Buddy's examination room. He never fixed the crack in his office door. When Buddy moved into his new office, he took the door with him. My hole remains on display today, serving as a continual reminder to those who come into Buddy's office that one defeat does not represent total failure.

Paul "Bear" Bryant once said, "The price of victory is high, but so are the rewards." Buddy, laughingly, has never let me forget my first experience with driving a wheelchair. Eighteen years later, he still kids me about that fiasco. I left his office that day bruised but not beaten, absolutely determined to show Buddy I could conquer that wheelchair.

Despite all of his encouragement, my body flew out of control too easily. There were other problems as well. My posture needed to be stabilized. The continual jerking of cerebral palsy does not permit me much control over my body when in a sitting position. I tend to slowly slump over to one side against my will. In order to exercise full control over a wheelchair joystick, I have to be sitting fully upright. Maintaining a steady left hand is hard enough without constantly having to reposition my body. My youngest brother, Ray, and I brainstormed and eventually came up with a creative idea.

We had found two old belts at home and conducted a little experiment. By strapping each leg just above the knee to its adjacent skirtguard, I was forced, rather painfully at first, to sit in an upright position. We first tried it out for five minutes. The excruciating pain reminded me all too clearly of my bracing days, but I knew as my ligaments stretched, it would get easier.

When I approached Buddy with the idea a month later, he was dead set against it. My legs, he concluded, were too tense to tolerate any additional stress. I had insisted that this was the only way, but Buddy would not be convinced until he saw the results. I began practicing strapping my legs at home, gradually building up enough tolerance until they could be strapped apart all day long. Today, this is only mildly uncomfortable, and I'll gladly trade a little irritation for the security of leg straps.

Eventually, I invested in two commercial leather dog collars. They generally last about a year, and I keep an extra set handy in case of an emergency.

The straps do more for me than maintaining my body alignment and supporting my posture. They keep me securely fastened to my wheelchair, acting as a kind of seat belt. I now felt secure in my wheelchair, and my deep-seated fear of falling out, which has happened on several occasions, no longer worries me like it used to. By applying the problem-solving skills Uncle Nora taught me long ago and using a little creativity, I overcame another obstacle on my road to independent living.

The next time I saw Buddy, when he was called in for consultation by Earnestine, he was forced to agree with evidence that there appeared to be improvement in my posture and body alignment. In fact, within a few months, my lower limbs had become more relaxed than they had ever been. Buddy decided the time had come for me to begin training for freedom: an electric wheelchair of my own. I felt a burst of unbridled energy shoot throughout my body until I laughed and cried with joy. Soon I would be able to explore the world alone.

My schooling in the art of wheelchair maneuvering began with observing Peter. He had been driving for about a year now and was damn good at it. Peter taught me how to gently caress the joystick. He said, "Touch the joystick the way you would a lady. Not too hard or soft, but just enough for stimulation."

Peter allowed me to tap his joystick, while alongside his chair. His coaching helped me to become comfortable with the mechanics of driving. From May until October, we practiced together. It was time for the third IEP meeting with Buddy and Earnestine. They both felt I had gained enough control to take my second driving test. This time was for keeps. If I passed, my new wheelchair would become a reality.

Buddy decided the parking lot was a much safer place to conduct the test. We went through a series of exercises, during which I moved forward and backward, turned left and right, even parallel parked, all with complete success. Crossing the street and moving up a handicap accessible ramp proved to be slightly more difficult but manageable. Dr. Holder and Buddy were very much impressed, and I received my license to drive! My first electric wheelchair, an Everest and Jennings Premiere, came through Mary Williams, our rehabilitation counselor/facilitator assigned to WACS by the state.

An electric wheelchair is like a car in many respects. Maintenance and repair are equally as expensive as taking your car to a mechanic. A word of caution to those of you who have just received your first electric chair: Never let your chair become an instrument of play; they are expensive, and the majority are paid for with our tax dollars. Respect and tend to your chair, because when treated right it will take excellent care of you.

My motorized wheelchair is an extension of my body . . . my legs, if you will. I hope that people will learn to focus more on me and not on my wheelchair. I have accepted my role in a wheelchair as an emblem of strength, an integral part of my life. Peter Moore once said, "I know that God put me in a chair to represent His good works on Earth. If I must be confined, let it be a mobile confinement."

The Promise Kept

June 5, 1979, was a notably triumphant day for me. It was my first day of classes as an official, verifiable student at the University of Alabama. When Johnny Nash, our faithful bus driver and aide at WACS, wheeled me through the doors of New College for my first day of class in NEW 222, Academic Potential, a new world unfolded before me. The class lasted about an hour, after which my instructor rolled me outside to await Johnny's return. I was overcome with feelings of miraculous accomplishment. As I allowed my gaze to roam across the quad, my thoughts began to drift. I looked upwards and declared:

"Milton, this is for you. I made it, my brother, I finally succeeded. With God's help and you, I got my GED, and into college. Thank you."

The following weeks were grueling, and they passed quickly. NEW 222 was a pass/fail class, and I came out of first summer session smelling like a rose. I took two classes during the next semester. The first was Social Science I and the other was a special class on my disability, which I took with Peter, called The Oak Hill Institute in Cerebral Palsy. Peter and I gave a presentation on the social aspects of being disabled during the second week of class.

After the joint lecture, a young woman named Gwendolyn Peabody (not her real name) came up and introduced herself to us. She had recently changed her major to special education from physical management, and, greatly inspired by what we had shared with the class, she wanted to get to know us better. Peter and I were only too happy to oblige.

Second summer session was another rung on my educational ladder. I earned an A in my class on cerebral palsy, and I passed Social Science I. My life was at a peak of contentment, and I was infatuated. Her name was Barbara Fosters. What a knockout! A practicum student at WACS, majoring in multiple disabilities, Barbara grabbed my fancy by the throat and proceeded to form a choke hold.

I took my classes very seriously, but Barbara's presence made it really difficult to look at a book. She was an incredibly beautiful athletic-type girl, and I gave her a run for her money. I mean literally, as in chased her around the room once I got my electric chair! She was thin, about 5' 9", with long, flowing brunette hair and flecked-blue eyes. You know the type, the kind of girl that causes traffic accidents on college campuses.

Dr. Holder watched our relationship develop with guarded optimism, but when she caught us laughing and goofing off one day with Barbara sitting in my lap, while we were supposed to be studying, she decided enough was enough. "This kind of behavior," Dr. Holder explained, "cannot be tolerated between my practicum students and clients in the WACS program. The university could be held accountable for any deviant activities between you two occurring while at the center. What you do in your own time, however, is your own business." Barbara looked at me, I smirked back, and each of us knew what the other was thinking; we set a date for lunch at the Ferguson Center cafeteria in a couple of days.

For those of you who may not remember your first date or what you were feeling at the time, allow me to refresh your memory: "Oh, no! I have nothing to wear . . . where's my comb?" and constant butterflies in the stomach, to boot. "What if she doesn't like me? What if she does? What am I to do if things go sour? Where will I run off to?"

I couldn't very well get up and leave the table! My electric chair was still on order from Los Angeles at this time. Once the two of us were alone together, I couldn't go anywhere without her help. Uncle Nora watched my fretfulness with humorous knowing. Thank goodness he came to my rescue.

"Nate, you got to remember dat chou ain't no man about town yet."

"What do you mean by that?"

"I mean, you got to treat dis here girl like a flower. You cain't go pickin' her petals; not just yet, son. Not just yet. You've got to treat her delicately. If you fail in the attempt, she will crush in your hands. What I'm sayin' is dis, treat Barbara with respect, and you will get the same."

Together that morning, we rummaged through my meager wardrobe to select suitable attire for this momentous occasion. What we came up with still amuses me today. Uncle Nora, expert on early seventies fashion coordinating and lady killing, came up with quite a dapper outfit. He pulled a pair of forest green polyester slacks, and a one hundred percent cotton, matching green, Arrow button-down short sleeve shirt from the depths of the family closet. Ray spent over half an hour styling my afro to my satisfaction. When the project was complete, my hair mused out three inches in all directions. I knew I was looking good, but in the house there was a difference of opinion.

"Boy, what's wrong wit' chour head? You look like a mop!"

"Momma, Joyce, Sam, you all don't know what's happenin', right, Uncle?"

"Y'all lookin' at Joe College, in a wheelchair no less!"

I was meticulous with everything that morning; bathroom, breakfast, and travel, nothing was going to hinder the pending moment. At WACS everyone, especially Peter, was janking on me. They were all green with envy, almost as green as I was! Barbara was, without a doubt, the most stunning lady who had ever graced the halls of the center to date. When the hour of reckoning was close at hand, Johnny took me over to the Ferguson Center for my date with destiny.

My palms began to sweat as we entered the building. Every time I get really anxious, my cerebral palsy kicks in, causing unwanted body movement. In this case, my right arm, which tends to jerk about under extreme duress, began to flail wildly. Quickly, I seized it with my left hand, pulling it down until it looked like my hands were comfortably crossed in my lap. "No need to appear nervous," I thought to myself. The tension mounted as we rounded the corner.

There she was, a radiant goddess amidst the humdrum inhabitants who usually frequent the Terrace Cafeteria. Wearing a lovely white, intricately embroidered cotton sundress, Barbara was truly a vision to behold. She smiled as I approached, and said, "Nathan, you look really nice today."

"Thank you, Barbara."

"May I ask you something personal?"

"Of course."

"How do you feel, when people stare at you?"

I understood this line of questioning intimately. To the immediate right of our table, there sat an elderly balding man, and the dullard was gawking rudely at us. I can only imagine what he must have been thinking, seeing a disabled black man with such a gorgeous white girl. Barbara put her elbows on the table, and with her chin resting between each of her palms, stared back at the man with a mirror of his own expression. The man scoffed and left in a huff, while we laughed in delight!

Barbara wanted to assist me in eating my food, but I would not allow it. I had spent the last five years of my life preparing for this moment and was not about to appear any less capable than her. She understood my feelings completely. As we ate together, salad, roast beef, and broccoli for her, and fried chicken with mashed potatoes for me, we had a very pleasant discussion.

She was greatly enjoying a class on multiple disabilities. Her experiences at WACS had given her a deeper understanding of life for people with exceptionality. After our meal, we sat around and sipped our drinks, sweetened ice tea for her and an orange soda for me, until Johnny came to pick me up. I got a great big bear hug from Barbara before she left for her next class. I felt whole, like I had come out of a pool clean, renewed, and full of newfound energy.

I will never forget Barbara. We shared some really special times. My first date reminded me, despite my physical disability, beautiful women still can have a genuinely good time with me. Barbara stayed at WACS until the end of the semester, after which I saw her off and on until her marriage and her move to somewhere in Georgia. Times change though, and these days my social life is pretty extensive.

My Chariot

On October third my chariot arrived! Buddy Mason had it delivered to the center as soon as it came in. When Johnny strapped me in, my life immediately took on a new perspective. I was mobile, and everyone, including Peter Moore, shared in my delight. It felt good just to be able to move independently, without someone always pushing me from behind. It was like that constant companion I always had suddenly vanished forever. I was ecstatic and couldn't wait to show Nora, Momma, and the rest of the family.

Earnestine called ahead to make certain the door was wide enough. A doorway must be at least thirty-two inches across, or wider, if a chair of that magnitude is to fit through it. A makeshift ramp would have to be rigged, supporting at least two hundred extra pounds. Momma remedied the situation immediately, by uncovering an old door she kept out back for just such an occasion. Back at the center, I was eager to get outside and try out my new wheels.

Johnny and Peter helped me get adjusted to my new mobility. Peter taught me how to maneuver over rough terrain and come up a hill without overturning the chair. Driving one of these babies is not as easy as it looks. It's a game of balance and precision, to be played with the highest degree of safe conduct. One screw-up in traffic, for example, could result in death. Both Johnny and Peter emphasized the importance of taking time to learn about the mechanics of driving before cruising around town.

"Do you remember our comparison between a lady and the joystick? Here's an example, Nathan. Hit the joystick with a heavy hand. Do it gently and swiftly. Good! Do you see how it took off like a jet and threw your head back? That is called inertia. It works on a principle of action versus opposite reaction. You've got to prepare yourself to be thrown off balance. That way you can recover all the more swiftly."

Next, he had me practice until I could ease the chair into motion without wrenching my body into an awkward position. I found that the key lies in how one manipulates the joystick. It sits in the center of my control box, identical to that of a video game. Similarly, it can be tilted in any direction. Apply a slight amount of pressure in any direction, and the chair clicks, then moves in the direction of joystick extension at any given moment. Movement speed is variant according to how far in that direction the joystick is extended: slight for slight motion, more for speed. It's all in the wrist.

The other key element to wheelchair driving is body position in relation to the location of the control box. It varies according to one's respective disability. In my case, the upright position is ideal. I have no control over my right arm and hand, and only partial movement and control of my left arm and hand. I had to drive with my first two fingers and thumb, at first, but now I can use my whole hand. Since my left arm will almost fully extend, and it has to be that way the entire time I operate the chair, it is crucial that my body sits as straight as possible.

That's where my leg straps come into play. With their help, I can lean into any of a variety of positions and straighten myself successfully. Their most important benefit, though, is that they offer balance. Going up and down a hill requires perfect equilibrium.

Traveling uphill, I extend the joystick straight out in front of me and lean forward as much as possible, until the majority of my body weight is above the center of gravity. Otherwise, the chair would be unable to overcome the resulting friction, and be left with its wheels spinning to no avail. Downhill, the center of gravity is at the rear of the chair. I have to pull the joystick straight back to reduce speed, which increases rapidly otherwise. This does no damage to the gears or motor since the wheelchair is powered electrically. Then, I lean back until most of my body weight is over the back wheels, in order to keep from turning the chair over forward.

After two and a half hours, I felt comfortable enough with my driving abilities to head home. Momma and Ray were awaiting my arrival. They had the ramp all ready to go. The door fit over the stairs exactly and at a suitable angle: forty-five degrees. Johnny dropped me off, and watched as I drove up the ramp. It felt funny to me, driving up that unsteady contraption, but I had little difficulty.

Momma looked out the window and declared in astonishment, "Nathan, I don't believe it. You are actually drivin' a motorized wheelchair! Ray! Come here and look at chour brother!" I grinned ear to ear, as they cleared the way for me to get inside. Later that afternoon, I took Ray with me to show Nora and Annie Bell. Ray couldn't believe the speed of my chair. He had to run, just to keep up. Remembering the advice of my friends, I slowed down to keep from having an accident.

Uncle and Auntie were unequivocally impressed, "Nate, we are so proud of you for getting this chair. It will make your life a lot easier and show people you have come full circle." Uncle Nora gave me a big hug, and said, "Now, son, you have a responsibility to keep this chair in workin' condition. It will take care of you, because it is yo' legs." Ray looked at Nora and agreed.

Things were difficult, to begin with, at home. The furniture had to be rearranged in such a way as to allow me access to every room in the house. Momma, though a bit nervous at first, was very proud of me.

"Nathan, be careful when you go outside because there are holes in de street dat will cause you to turn over."

"I will be extremely careful, and if I get in trouble, I will let somebody know I need assistance."

It was exhilarating! After years of being pushed, to suddenly be alone to explore the world around me. I was aching to go out on the town. After

Momma's advice, I drove to the park, about a block away, to check out the scene. I wasn't looking for anyone in particular, just the opportunity to be alone somewhere.

Many of the neighborhood kids saw me, and they ran like hell at the sight of me rolling down the road! I was a sight to behold, for none of them had witnessed a motorized wheelchair before. For that matter, almost none of my friends and acquaintances in Northport had either. Shock, disbelief, laughter, and delight were often among the first reactions I got from people. What fun it was, too. I was finally "one of the boys."

I used my wheelchair to attend all of my classes. Johnny was no longer required to ensure I would get from one class to another. Now, with my "electronic legs," Peter and I both had the means to succeed. We had the means to become everything we ever wanted to be, and that was the plan. I passed every class I took fall semester, earning an A in "Exceptional Child/Youth."

Peter and I took Social Science II together, and I did so well that Dr. Rosenberg gave me his congratulations. Peter and I studied together for all of the classes that we took together or separately. My life, however, was changing dramatically. I had been, for some time now, drifting apart from my friends and surrogate family at the center. Gwendolyn Peabody and I were quickly becoming a team.

Over the summer of 1979, she volunteered to take me around Tuscaloosa County, to places I had never been before. Baskin-Robbins Ice Cream Store, for example, had been completely unknown to me. Similarly, University Mall, Lake Tuscaloosa, and Kentuck Park were all new to me. I found Kentuck Park to be artistically stimulating. At the park there is a festival every fall, the highlight of October for the local populace, where arts and crafts are displayed, created by people from a variety of southern states and beyond.

Gwendolyn was the first new friend I'd found in a long time. She was also fairly wealthy and not hesitant to spend her money on me. I loved the attention, and I loved her, as a friend. Under Uncle Nora's watchful eye, we learned to enlarge each other's horizons.

After the summer of 1979, I never had another class with Gwendolyn Peabody, but I saw more of her than ever. She became involved with WACS as a practicum student in the fall and became close friends with Dr. Holder as time progressed. Gwendolyn was generous enough to loan me $500.00, interest-free money, to cover the cost of my fall semester tuition. I was eligible for a Pell Grant again, but Momma wouldn't sign the paperwork describing my family's financial situation. I tried to explain to her, the university wasn't being nosey, "this is the procedure for everybody in college," but she wouldn't understand.

Many things took place that fall, besides my enrollment in four classes. Earnestine left at the end of August. Her replacement's name was Pat Evans. Gwendolyn and I began work on my book, on September 18, 1979. That same semester, I met several other new friends who introduced me to campus life: fraternity parties, concerts, sports, all of that good stuff. College was an explosion of new information, and a massive culture shock. Now that I had wheels, I was ready to conquer the world. As it turns out, many swift changes of fate were rapidly approaching.

Sitting Alone

Pat Evans came to WACS with a teaching degree in psychology. Besides being a teacher, she was our counselor and confidante. Pat brought new dynamics to the program and a passionate sense of humor. As she watched our antics, which became more evident to her over time, she found them to be both amusing and amazing.

"You and your damn independence!" she would exclaim, every time we would question her analytical perspective of us. It became apparent to her immediately, we were not the type of people who conform to the mold. Peter and I were advancing much faster in our academic pursuits than Snow, but we never forgot that he was a genius of sorts.

Snow is a whiz at math. The boy is awesome. He could figure things out then that remain foreign to me now. In fact, Snow earned his GED in 1997. Snow, Peter, and I talked about the future and what it would entail for the three of us. Little did we know then what kind of changes lay ahead. Swift, drastic changes would devastate our universe like a mighty earthquake very soon.

I discovered Aaron Dobbyne during Dr. Jerry Rosenberg's class, Man In Society. Aaron was a freshman and had ambitions of being an Alabama basketball star. He and I became good friends, as he helped me with note-taking and I listened to his dreams. He was like a brother to me, and I hope he is doing well. He wanted, more than anything else, to be respected as an articulate and intellectual man. It's difficult for a black man to earn respect, and that was more important to him than anything else.

As fate would have it, Aaron never made the team, but he did graduate from college. He's a Baptist minister in Selma, Alabama, today. He has the respect of his congregation and the community. I miss him. Soon after we met, I needed a friend pretty badly.

One February night in 1980, Peter and his mother returned home from a nightclub where the soul band she managed had been playing. Things were kind of tense at home for Peter's sister, Rhonda. She had recently broken up with her boyfriend. He was a real maniac, the kind of gangster your mother warns you to avoid.

That very evening, the distraught young man lay in wait for them. He busted through the door about five minutes after Peter and his mother arrived home, wielding a powerful handgun and blaming Peter's mother for his breakup with Rhonda. She stood in front of her son's wheelchair, blocking Peter from potential harm at the hands of this lunatic. Everyone was screaming: his mother at the deranged man, the man at her, Rhonda to no one in particular.

Peter was in shock, when suddenly the man took aim and fired at his mother, penetrating her chest cavity. She fell back into Peter's lap and, looking into his eyes with a long, mournful, powerless stare of confusion and helplessness, died in his blood-soaked arms. The man turned the gun on Rhonda and fired again, seriously wounding her, but she would recover. With the sirens already wailing far in the distance, the man fled. He is now serving a life sentence for premeditated murder, but Peter Moore was never the same again.

Peter was a comfort to me when Milton died. When I thought my life was over, Peter told me, "You can't look at death from a living perspective. We have to look at death from a higher plane." I tried, with my heart and soul, to impress the same message onto him. He did not know how to go on, and for the first time since I'd known him, Peter was at a loss for words.

There are no words to describe what happened. Murder is a hardship no one should have to endure, but in my community, it is terrifyingly frequent and often goes unnoticed by the general populace. Peter's anger and feelings of inadequacy swallowed him up. This is the most difficult thing Peter ever had to face about himself. No one was ever able to convince him, not even me, that had he not been disabled, Peter still could not have saved his mother's life. He asked to withdraw and was released by the university from his spring schedule of classes.

Eaten up, inside and out, Peter never reacquired that spark of energy which had set him apart from all others. He did, however, go on with his life. Peter stayed a client at the WACS program but never went back to college. Education became unimportant on account of the loss he and his sister would now face and examine for the rest of their lives.

I visited Peter about three times a month during the years before his death at the hands of muscular dystrophy. We would talk about death, and what it meant to each of us. Peter died on a Saturday evening in late August of 1988. He was unable to care for himself in the last year. I think Peter lost a lot of his will to live much earlier, and if it weren't for his friends, he might not have made it as long as he did. I will always miss Peter Moore. He was my inspiration for many years, and most of all, he was my best friend.

During that unfortunate spring semester of 1980, I registered for some extremely difficult classes, and it became apparent to everyone that I was in over my head. Everyone but me, that is. Pat saw this fierce denial in me and tried to get me to realize hard classes and occasional bad grades were not a reflection on my intelligence. This was especially true as she and Dr. Holder took into account the effect Peter's catastrophe had on me. I had agreed, at Peter's insistence, to stay in school despite my desire to spend all of my time comforting my friend.

I felt worse than stupid. I really believed myself to be a complete idiot. "I made an A on that last test," is about all Holder or anyone else could get out of me. The truth is, I had become scared of college and was too afraid to admit it to myself. My classes, so easy for me before, had become insurmountable barriers. I began to wonder if for the first part of my college career, I had just chanced upon some easy classes. In truth, my educational travails were for a variety of reasons.

My sister, Jean, had moved back from Detroit and into our house in the middle of spring semester, about one month before Peter's tragedy. Let me make it perfectly clear: Jean has never, not even when we were little, been able to understand my relationship with Momma. Caring for me has always required a lot of time, and some of my siblings feel like they missed out on Momma's attention. This is commonplace in any household with a disabled youth. From the first day Jean moved back in, trouble began brewing.

She appeared tolerant at first, exactly what I had hoped. Jean moved into her old bedroom. This would pose a problem because, in order to get to the kitchen, I would have no alternative but to go through Jean's room. The only other entrance to the kitchen was blocked by the bed Ray slept on. I knew this would eventually cause problems, but Jean's true feelings toward me erupted with a vengeance sooner than I anticipated. She was back to her childhood cruelty the first time I tried to pass through her room. SLAM!!

"Momma, he ain't coming through my room and scarring up my furniture with his wheelchair!"

"But dat is the only way he can get though to the kitchen!"

"Why can't I come through your room? I won't mess up your furniture."

"Everything you touch, Nathan, you mess it up!"

"Let Nathan pass through dis room so he kin eat his dinner!"

I was eventually able to pass through her room, but only because Jean respected Momma. I was an altogether different story. Her open hatred blazed forth and began to manifest itself in unspeakable ways. Jean abused me mentally, physically, and emotionally.

The abuse continued through the next year, and ended up with me in the hospital. What you are about to read is not make-believe, and incredulous as it may seem, I hold no malice in my heart for Jean. Instead, Jean did me a big favor. She mistreated me enough to tell the truth, and I forgive her for everything. Understand, this kind of thing happens all the time to people with disabilities, as well as children, the elderly, and the infirm.

From my viewpoint, abusers see no wrong in their actions. All they see is putting the abusee, who is "nothing but trouble," in his or her place. Very often, as with Jean, an abuser has been abused as well, somewhere in their past. It has got to stop somewhere, and a good step toward understanding this all too common nightmare is through public deliberation to comprehensively frame the nature of the problem.

The room incidents were merely an annoyance, and I was always fed anyway; Momma made sure of that. She may not have believed everything, but she always jumped to my defense. It started a few days after Jean moved in. Momma and I were sitting on the front porch when I asked for a glass of water. She yelled inside, "Jean, bring Nathan a glass of water, please." She sure enough did, but from around the corner where Momma couldn't see, though Jean made sure I could, she spit in the water. When she came outside and handed it to me, I told Momma what had happened. Of course, Jean denied it, but I threw it down and refused to drink it. Momma fetched me another.

The next time was about six months later. Jean may not have done anything else during that difficult semester, but the hateful ambiance and constant harassment did nothing to enhance my study environment. I either withdrew or received incompletes for all of my classes that spring except for one, Fundamentals of Speech, in which I received a C. Dr. Holder and everyone else at the center knew what was going on at home, but there wasn't anything they could do about it. I underwent psychological counseling to combat the depression that plagued my life and to find a method of venting my ever-growing frustration.

One evening in May, Momma asked Jean to assist me in eating. She sat down beside me with a steaming plate of food. Being the trusting soul I am, I opened my mouth to receive a tempting morsel. She shoved a piece of piping hot cornbread into my mouth, scalding the whole inside, roof, tongue, cheeks, and all. I screamed like a wounded animal, spitting cornbread everywhere, as she snickered gleefully.

Momma refused to believe me as I tried to explain, in between sobs, what had just transpired. As usual, Jean played the part of an innocent victim of my outlandish accusations. Finally, a few weeks ago, Momma and I had a long talk about those days. Looking back, she will admit Jean's abhorrent treatment of me and regrets the way she handled the situation. I can't eat hot food, even today. I want to relearn how to, but the burns were so bad and the blisters hurt for so long, I live in fear of ever being burnt like that again. Room temperature or cold food is all I put in my mouth today.

Jean saw what she could get away with after the cornbread incident. She made it clear to me, if Momma died before I did, she would ensure my placement in a state facility. Today, the law still has allowances for this kind of practice in the disabled community, when disabled involvement in community affairs is so crucial to understanding our contributive value. An individual who has been labeled mentally retarded, or with any developmental disabilities, can be easily placed in a nursing home today. It doesn't matter what intellectual capabilities they possess, or what their status is as a legal adult, families can institutionalize someone against their will.

There are ways to challenge this practice now. I will get into more detail about how the principles behind the Americans with Disabilities Act could be expanded in the future. It is an excellent first step toward protecting people like me and giving a method of defense against anyone who tries to violate the civil rights of citizens with exceptionality.

The Beginning of Hell

Things were getting progressively worse and I struggled to maintain my sanity. The stress at home reached a point where I lost my whole identity. Jean was beating on me, literally slapping me and hitting me with a switch. Her attacks seemed to blame me for some pain inside of her, but it manifested in ways which influenced my self-image. I began to doubt myself, because Jean would humiliate me, and I had to put up with her continual attempts to exercise control over every facet of my home life.

In the summer I passed both of my classes, with a C in Educational Psychology, and a D in Biology, if you call that passing. Uncle Nora and my friends at the center tried to comfort me. The despair I felt over Peter, my struggles with college, and the mental and physical abuse at home enveloped me. Depression consumed me. For the first time in my life, even Uncle Nora could not reach me.

I visited him one afternoon that dark summer after returning home from the center. Uncle Nora was sitting out in his yard. He saw me coming up the street, as I often did to escape the tension at home, and helped me into the yard. Though the cherry tree had been chopped down a year ago, its stump remained as a symbol of my roots, planted under that old tree many years ago. We sat outside, and conversed for hours.

Nora recognized something startling in my appearance and manner. Hearing an unfamiliar sound in my voice, one of despair and a plea for help, he did his best to encourage me. "You and I, Nate, ain't no quitters. No matter what chour sister is doin' to you son, you gotta reach way down within' yo'self, and tap into dat energy we all get from a higher source den ourselves."

His words were affecting me, but I was past all hearing, beyond all faith. I felt like I'd put forward my best, and someone had mutilated it before my eyes.

During this time, I wanted so badly to get out, somewhere other than Tuscaloosa. My travels in the past years had planted a seed. The experiences of Florida, Washington, Louisville, and New Orleans taught me there existed a plethora of new places and friendly faces, beyond the seeming prison of my hometown. Everyone at the center was concerned about me because they all knew things were worse than I would let on. Things were bad enough already, and getting more tiresome all the time.

Pam Smith was our newest teacher in the fall, replacing Pat Evans. I would blame Pam for part of my dilemma, at that time. She vigorously insisted, "There is no obstacle you cannot overcome." Then she proceeded to show each of the clients at WACS, but especially Peter, Snow, and myself, how this was true in our individual lives. In my case, she frankly recommended I face my inability to handle things as well as I thought I could and slow down my momentum.

This was not something I wanted to hear. It came to me as an insult from the support base I counted on the most. Of course, Pam had no idea what was happening at home; only Dr. Holder had that information. Pam only saw me struggling with a school schedule I could not manage and witnessed a rapid deterioration of my spirit. She correctly interpreted my lack of enthusiasm for the activities at WACS to be a cry for help. She merely misunderstood the direction from which it was coming.

Pam wanted me to take some time off from school because she thought my course load too burdensome for me. It's true, I was giving up, not because of school, but because brutality and destructiveness engulfed my domestic life. Though she had no way of knowing about this, I did not care and was insulted to the point of fury. I believed my family at WACS was now pulling the rug out from under me, and I felt cornered into lies and deception.

Let me explain. Along with many other people who have grown up under exceedingly stressful circumstances, I am a survivor. I have always felt the need to appear, even when it was not necessarily so, that I'm better off than I really am. When trapped into sacrificing the things which I feel encompass my manhood, I get scared to extremes. Things like my education, my apartment, this book, my motorized wheelchair, my friends and loved ones, I will not compromise on. I will not back down. To quit school would be backing down, and I would not then; and after twelve years of struggle, I will not now.

I may be wrong, but that is how I perceived the situation to be one Wednesday in late October of 1981, when Pam told me to drop my classes for fall semester. I retorted, "The hell I will!" Around this same time Dr. Holder hired an administrative assistant to help her effectively conduct business in the face of an expanding WACS program and a full teaching schedule. Her name was Sallie Reader, and she watched the developing turmoil carefully.

Earlier in October had been my midterm exams. I failed all three of them miserably. Philosophy 100 required massive reading and note-taking skills. "Abnormal Psychology" and "Child Psychology" both had similar requirements. I'm embarrassed to admit it, but I don't have these skills. I do have an effective way of taking notes; my tape recorder serves me well—but in order to organize the information, I would need a computer, too expensive for somebody like me at that time, or some other method of organizing notes, making outlines, things of that nature.

I had two practicum students that semester to aid me in completing assignments. Crystal and Vickie were both helpful, but only up to a point. I was ashamed to let anyone on to the fact that I was not able to do it on my own, whether it was making flashcards, writing a paper, or organizing things. No one, I might add, took the time to explain to me when such things would be required or that no one innately understands how to study. I assumed, wrongly, that I was just supposed to "know" how to be a good student, and my mediocre reading skills didn't help.

NEW 222 was a chance I missed to develop these skills, but it was not geared for my needs. "Academic Potential," as the New College studies skills course is titled, was designed to improve writing skills and to teach how to more effectively take handwritten notes in class. How is that going to benefit me? I can't write anything by hand but my name! I passed NEW 222, along with everyone else who takes that class, based on my attendance and effort. That's how a study skills class has to be graded, because everyone starts, and ends up, on different ability levels.

I am perfectly capable of grasping each and every technicality involved in college study, once the vocabulary is clear to me, but it was plainly evident that without the note-taking skills I would not be able to continue my studies. I reverted to childhood trickery, just like the "Dry Rot Syndrome" of old.

Knowing I was on the verge of collapse, I fought with every inch of fiber in me. I devised a fruitless scheme to help me escape my pain. Uncle Nora knew my trips to the library were not to study psychology and saw all my new talk about transferring to Texas A&M for what it was, a bunch of malarkey. He'd seen me fabricating absurd stories as a child, and with characteristic patience, he called my bluff. "Nate, I know you are hurting, but dere's no reason for you to lie like this to people who love you."

"I am not lyin' to you, Uncle Nora."

"Who in de hell do you think I am, boy?"

"I know who you are, Uncle."

"I don't think so."

"You are mad at me, aren't chou?"

"No, Nate, I am jus' disappointed in you. Because I know you know the right thing to do, I jus' don't understand why you are so afraid to do it. I will love you unconditionally, son. You are hurtin', and I know dis."

As he spoke, I stared off into space, withdrawing into myself more and more, because I was unable to accept that my problems with school were not my fault. I couldn't even share my feelings of inadequacy with him, and that was bad. Pam and Dr. Holder became very concerned about me, and very suspicious. Upon discovering my miserable midterm grades, Dr. Holder called me into her office for a conference between herself, Sallie, and me. I was feeling pretty abysmal rolling into her office.

She had noticed a marked change in my attitude toward everyone at the center, especially herself, and asked me what was wrong. I blew up in her face and denied everything, calling my teachers crazy, the center useless, and accusing Dr. Holder of not being my friend anymore. I told them I was transferring somewhere better than the University of Alabama. My shenanigans were now ready for revelation.

I informed Dr. Holder of the excellent psychology program at Texas A&M and that the campus was completely accessible to the disabled. I had spent many hours in preparation for this moment, knowing Dr. Holder would eventually discover I was failing out of school. I had even learned the name of a friend of hers who taught in the special education department at Texas A&M, Tom, and told her I would be taking one of his classes. My snow job of Dr. Holder was detailed and calculated.

I agreed that things were not good. I blamed my problems with school on the mistreatment at home, which they all knew was bad. Perhaps a new environment would be good for me, everyone thought, and I had told them I would be getting my own dorm room. After some discussion, I agreed to drop Philosophy 100; I had the lowest grade in there, anyway. Psychology classes were another matter, and I was determined to pass both of those classes despite problems at home or the fact that both grades were very low at midterm. Sallie, Dr. Holder, Pam, and the others felt this was a fair compromise.

I did my best to pull out both grades, studying intensely and attending every class, but I only managed to pass "Child Psychology." Everyone at the center was impressed with that much, considering the fact that Jean was leaving noticeable bruises on my body by the end of fall semester, and everyone at WACS wanted to know the details. Only Dr. Holder knew the truth, and it placed her in a precarious situation. Her first impulse was to press charges, but were she to do that, Momma would likely withdraw me from the program.

After much thought, and a lot of gut-wrenching, we decided the best thing to do would be to let things lie. The unstable situation at home would kill me, were it not for the WACS program, and she knew it. Besides, Dr. Holder did not want to lose me to those who could not recognize the progress I was making for what it was. I would never become independent if I left the center.

Instead, she had me receive counseling under Bill Wysinger. Together, we explored alternative methods of dealing with stress. He mainly tried to keep me from collapsing. Despite everything we did, my walls of endurance were crumbling. Bill saw signs in me of something much worse than depression, and this troubled him greatly.

Fading Fast

I was in for the biggest fight of my life. Against the advice of everyone, I registered for twelve hours spring semester of 1982: College Algebra, Natural Science II, Developmental Psychology, and Psychology of Law and Justice. I knew this would be too much, but if I was going to sink, I figured I might as well drown. Have you ever felt like you've let everyone down? That's how I felt.

Milton, Uncle Nora, Dr. Mathews, Dr. Holder, and all those others who had put faith in me could never forgive me for failing out of school. I didn't realize, at that time, how easy it was to get overloaded; it happens to college students all the time. I thought once you failed, that was it. You were a failure. I felt like the biggest failure to set foot on the University of Alabama campus!

I fought to stay academically alive. Finding an advertisement for a math tutor hanging on a bulletin board in the Special Education Department, I called the girl, Jennifer, and she agreed to help me for a fee. I paid her five dollars an hour, and we met twice a week at my house in Northport. We studied together, and she helped me to grasp the fundamentals. I was doing well in College Algebra, maintaining a C average, but other classes weren't going as good. At midterm, I was passing everything but Natural Science II, my New College seminar with Dr. Blewitt.

The abuse at home reached a dangerous plateau. Under a hailstorm of verbal obscenities and continual threats, I managed to survive and even prosper academically, until one sour day in mid-March, when Jean went too far. Momma was in the kitchen cooking, when Jean came out into the living room, demanding I move out of her way, so she could get out the front door. When my wheelchair would not respond quickly enough for her, Jean spat, "You git outta my way!" Then, she kicked hard into my lower back.

Pain erupted from the bruised region, and I knew, as it spread, something was seriously wrong. I cried out to Momma, who rushed in to find me slumped over in agony. Coincidentally, I ended up in the hospital not even a week later with several kidney stones trying to pass through my urinary tract. I won't say that one is definitely related to the other, but the doctor suspected something recent must have dislodged the stones, triggering their release. Chances are, Jean's kick was at least a contributing factor.

I remained in the hospital for a week, and was laid up in bed at home for the next two weeks. The work I missed during this time was devastating to my hopes of keeping the difficult pace I had set at the beginning of the semester. I would have to withdraw, and it broke my spirit. Uncle Nora knew I was at my wit's end. He just tried to console me, "I know you don't believe this, Nate, but everything will be all right."

On February 4, 1982, all hell broke loose. Jean and another sister of mine named Sheila approached me, along with the rest of the family, demanding to know what had been written about them in my book. I wanted to share that information with them, but to be honest, it changed so frequently, I didn't even know what had been written. Were they mad? You bet.

To top it off, I arrived back at the center just in time for the cover to blow off my whole scheme. Dr. Holder had recently spoken with her friend Tom at Texas A&M and uncovered the truth that my "transfer" was a falsehood. When she told me this in her office, not even three days had passed since my return. Caught in a whirlwind of my own web of lies, and humiliated beyond all hope of recovery, I left her office. In the confused faces of my friends and comrades, I saw the same thing. "They all know! They know

I'm a failure!" I thought, as I rolled out the doors of WACS effusing tears, never intending to return. My pride made known lies as unacceptable as failure.

The next morning, when Johnny came to get me, I refused to go. "Tell Pam that I won't be coming back. I mean it! Go away!" He relayed the message to everyone back at WACS, and for several hours my phone rang off the hook, but I would speak with no one, not even Uncle Nora. My friends would not take "no" for an answer.

"Nathan, Dr. Mathews is on the phone. Will you take it?"

"Yes. I will take his call . . . Dr. Mathews?

"Nathan, I want you to help me with the implementation of these ramps around campus we've discussed."

"I don't know . . ."

"This would be a great favor to me, Nathan. I really need your help and input on this."

"All right. I'll do it."

Dr. Mathews contacted Melford Espy, the first chairman of the Architectural Barriers Committee. At eight o'clock the next morning, Melford assembled four disabled students, two wheelchair-bound, myself included, and two blind. Together with Melford, we were assigned to seek out and discover any and all barriers to disabled students we could find before four-thirty. We were quite a spectacle, the blind students pushing each wheelchair-bound student. I was depressed to the point where I preferred melancholy daydreaming to operating an electric chair.

One blind student pushed me off the curb despite my late and frantic pleas. I landed rather abruptly face down on University Boulevard. Someone from the engineering department was with us taking notes. He assisted Melford in getting me straightened out. Though slightly bitter, I smiled anyway, seeing the humor in our public spectacle.

Admittedly, this was exciting stuff. At the time, though, you couldn't have convinced me that any favor for a friend was worth getting bruised up over when I felt about a millimeter tall already. I believe these experiments eventually led to the development of an international design paradigm for all sidewalk access curbside ramps, developed through conscientious teamwork at the University of Alabama, under the auspices of David Mathews.

On Thursday of that same week, Sallie Reader came by the house. I guess she figured I would talk to her, having known her for only a few months. She was right.

"Why did you come here today, Sallie?"

"Because Dr. Holder and I . . . we are concerned about you, Nathan."

"I don't believe that for one damn minute."

"We can't condone your actions, but we do understand why you did it. Dr. Holder wants to see you again."

"You tell her for me that I don't want to see no damn body."

"What are you afraid of, Nathan?"

"I am not afraid of nuthin'!"

"May I ask you one last question before I go?"

"No. No, but chou gonna ask it anyway."

"Do you trust me?"

"Why should I trust you?"

"Everybody has let you down."

"Dat's right. You don't know how much."

"Peter said he's going to call you. Can I come back and see you again?"

"No."

For the next two weeks, I sank into a deep depression. I would not eat, I would talk to virtually no one. I stayed in my room with the door shut reading useless magazine articles and other insignificant junk. I stayed all by myself, away from even the television, which was located in the family room. If other people were going to be around me, I wanted no part of it.

About a day or two passed before I received a three-page letter from Gwendolyn. In the letter, she told me that she "feared" for me, and all about the "critical crossroads" I was at. She strongly encouraged me to find strength in *Courage Under Fire*, the book she had agreed to assist me in writing, suddenly named by her. That's right, she had already named my book! Her letter left me unaffected. I was completely without opinion, and it felt strangely heartening. This indifferent attitude multiplied to subsume every feeling I had about everything and everybody.

I was in my room wallowing when Uncle Nora came by Friday of the same week. As Momma described my condition, Nora became angry. He burst into the room, "Nate, what I am about to tell you, you may not wanna hear. You may not like it, and you may not speak to me, and when I'm finished I'm leaving."

"No!" I tried to exit the room. He caught my chair, whirled me around, and looked me dead in the eye.

"I won't let you cut yourself off from me. I need you."

"I am so tired of struggling and fighting. I just want to be left alone."

"Can't you realize that people like us cain't be givin' up? We got to go out there and keep fightin' for those who cain't fight for themselves!"

"After all what we've been through, what does it all mean, Nora? What does it all mean?"

"Do you remember when I tol' you dat God had somp'm special for you to do, son? Pull out that Bible . . . here in chapter three of Ecclesiastes it reads, 'To everything there is a season, and a time to every purpose under the heaven. . . .'

My higher purpose stood before me like an adversary imposing on all my schemes and self-pity. Uncle Nora made a mistake. Everything he said was true, but he took the wrong approach. I recognized my mission for what it was, but I felt as though I had failed in my mission! I shrank in fear from my duties; I cowered in the face of everything my life stands for today, and did then. No one could faze me. "Nathan Ballard, you are a complete failure," was ringing in my ears. Uncle Nora saw this too, and left in a huff, powerless against my own negative self-image.

Two days passed, and I remained unchanged. The only thing keeping me alive was my lack of effort to end it. I came to this realization on Sunday the twenty-third day of May, 1982. This day, as I thought about it, dropped me into the deepest despair I had ever experienced. On this very day, five years before, I had embarked upon my trip to represent the southeastern region of United Cerebral Palsy at the landmark conference in Washington. What a perfect day to kill myself.

Black Hole

It was about five o'clock in the evening. Momma left me alone while she and my stepfather, J.D., whom she met not long after my birth, went to the grocery store. I went into the kitchen, laid my head on the table, and began to cry miserably. As my tears fell, through bleary eyes I looked up to Heaven and asked God to take me away from all this. I was so tired and alone. Life had no meaning anymore. Neither did I, for that matter. My own education held no validity anymore. It was time to end it all. I reached over and opened a drawer to my left. Feeling around, I came across a wickedly sharp butcher's knife.

With a trembling hand, I fought my cerebral palsy until the blade ever-so-slightly nicked the wrist of my useless right arm. At the first sight of blood, I fainted, and the knife dropped to floor with a loud thump. About five minutes passed before I came to my senses. I sat in the kitchen and watched the light seep out of the sky. Remorseful, I pleaded with God, "Aid me. Give me strength to go on and help me to realize my place in this life. Help me to face Uncle Nora. I'm sorry."

The wound was bleeding, but, thank God, it was not nearly as serious as I had planned. This was my second chance, and I needed help. I needed to build my support base, so I could understand my worth better. Momma came home to find me in the kitchen with blood on my pants and arm. She found the knife down next to the pantry and began screaming at me, but I would say nothing.

I couldn't speak. I knew what had to be done. I went into my room and cleaned the wound myself. I was still bitter and wouldn't say a word to anyone, although they questioned me relentlessly.

About three days later, I got an unexpected visit. Sallie Reader did come back, and I thank God for her. Momma told Sallie what had transpired in the past days. She jumped on Sallie's case, blaming the center and Dr. Holder for all of my problems. If they hadn't put these ideas into my head, she maintained, I wouldn't be in this predicament now. Sallie took it all in stride. She merely asked permission to speak with me.

"Nathan, your momma told me about your attempt to kill yourself. Would you like to talk about it?""

"Yes, I would."

"Tell me, what is going through your head right now?"

"A lot of hurt and confusion."

"Confusion about what, Nathan?"

"Sallie, I don't know. I just know I'm confused."

"About WACS? Dr. Holder? Me? About your home life?"

"Stop trying to analyze me!"

"How can I even begin to analyze you, when you won't even talk to me?"

"I want you to leave, Sallie. Now."

"Before I leave, I've got one question to ask you."

"You had one last time. What is it?"

"Can I see you again?"

"Maybe."

Sallie did return, and as we spoke together over the next few weeks, I learned many things I had not been aware of. My friends at WACS had no idea what was going on. Dr. Holder, who also called periodically, had kept our meeting confidential. In other words, no one else knew I was not at Texas A&M! She reserved to me, and me alone, the right to tell anyone what was going on. Peter was very worried. I hadn't contacted him in weeks, and he knew something was fishy. Dr. Holder would tell him nothing except, between the two of them, I was at home. He agreed to keep this to himself, and he wanted to call me. It wasn't long before Peter came by the house, unannounced.

"Oh, you poor, poor little cripple. Up there wallowing in your own self-pity. What's wrong? You can't take it? Was all that talk you told me a lot of bullshit?"

"You git the hell outta my house, and don't chou ever come back here no more!"

"You sure you ain't too crippled to put me outta your house? Huh? Seriously, let's go outside and talk."

"I don't wanna go outside!"

"You damn sure need to go out because you look like hell warmed over."

Eventually, I gave in to Peter's insistence. Going outside was a big step for me. I hadn't been out of the house in over a month. He kicked my ass in gear real fast, scolding me for everything from my appearance to my regressed vocabulary. He put everything back into perspective, "Nathan, we can't let each other down. I don't know what's happened to you, but you are letting me down, now. You were there for me when my mother died. Let me be here for you now. You owe me that much, Nate."

I was on the road to recovery. As soon as I felt strong enough, I went to see Uncle Nora and Auntie. When he saw me coming, Uncle Nora ran out and hugged me tightly, stating firmly, "There's nothing to be said." That was the end of it.

My uncle had limitless patience. Auntie expressed similar feelings. She knew what it was like to lose everything and get it back again. During the next few months, Nora, Peter, Gwendolyn, and especially Sallie helped me regain my self-esteem and confidence. I am eternally grateful.

In November, I wrote Dr. Holder a long letter, with the help of Sallie, who was visiting about twice a week. In the letter I asked her forgiveness for all I had done. I also asked, when I felt strong enough, could I return to the WACS program? Pam and Dr. Holder were elated!

They told me to take my time and return whenever I was ready. The next time we spoke, in February of 1983, I asked to return at the beginning of

March. Dr. Holder was thrilled to have me back, but not nearly as happy as I was to be returning.

On March 8, 1983, the bus pulled up to my house, and Johnny loaded me up. It was good to see Johnny. In fact, it was good to see everybody, and for the first time in over a year, we were on our way to the center. The family was whole again, and I had a great deal of unfinished business to tend to.

Pam was waiting at the door with a big bear hug. We had a long talk. During the passing weeks, I readjusted to the schedule at the center, but I did not register for classes. The university, it turns out, had suspended me. I received failing grades or incompletes for spring semester of 1982. I am still in the process of remedying that situation today, by finishing incomplete work, so that I may receive passing grades for some of those old courses.

Gwendolyn was delighted to see me and anxious to get back working on my book. She and I worked diligently together, doing the research, interviews, and actual writing over the next year, with her acting as my hands, or "ghostwriter." Jean moved out of the house in July and into her own apartment. Thank God for that.

Things were looking up, and the book was nearing completion, in first draft, by October of 1983. I was in the limelight and, thanks to Mary Jo Deaver, we even had an editor and publisher! His name was Jim Travis, the owner of Portals Press. Following the chaos which ensued shortly after his arrival on the scene, I was ready to launch the book into high gear, as soon as it was humanly possible.

PART THREE

Recess Is Over!!

Wealth Beyond Measure

Jim Travis was a former senior editor at the University of Alabama Press. He saw immediately that Gwendolyn's writing was inadequate and invited me to his house in late August of 1983 to discuss publication of *Courage Under Fire*. This upset Gwendolyn tremendously. I think she knew what he was going to tell me that night.

"You've got to get rid of Gwendolyn. Her writing ability is lacking in everything. I recommend Mary Jo Deaver."

"Jim, I know that Gwendolyn can do the job. Please give her a chance to prove herself."

We entered into a heated debate, during which I informed him of all the wonderful things that were developing in my life, thanks to her. He told me, although she may be a terrific person, she can't effectively express feeling on paper. In short, he was saying to me, Gwendolyn is no writer. Coming from a man of his credentials, I was forced to admit he was probably right. This put me in a very precarious position. How do you tell your friend that she can't write your life story, considering all the work we had already done?

Despite all my praises of Gwendolyn, the family still questioned our relationship. It was around this time Uncle Nora warned me, "Nate, remember: Everything that shines ain't gold. Watch, as well as pray." Gwendolyn bought me all kinds of items, but the most important thing I had was her friendship, which was more valuable than anything else she could ever buy or give me. I was unwilling to suspect anything because of all the nice things she was doing for me, like giving me clothes, a wristwatch, artwork, music, jewelry, even a new radio/tape deck!

I put myself on the line by asking Gwendolyn to at least consider letting Mary Jo help us organize material. She vehemently refused. The more I tried to work with Jim, the more insistent he got about Gwendolyn, who did everything she could to produce the kind of work that would make Jim proud of her. He admired her and respected her very much, but they had irreconcilable differences.

Time passed, and when we completed our first draft on October 25, 1983, it was a momentous occasion for the project. After four years of research, struggle, and accomplishment, we had completed our work. We went to the office of Alabama Disabilities Advocacy Program, to have an agreement—not a legal contract—drawn up that would set these arrangements in stone. She was, in all three drafts of this agreement, the ghostwriter. I would have full editorial control.

With all the bickering and textual changes going on, I wondered what exactly we had done. It dawned on me, as I thumbed through the text alone one afternoon, that my autobiography was becoming more a textbook on disability than a story about me. Much of the material and its phrasing was foreign to me.When I asked Gwendolyn what the book said about my family, she encouraged me to "seek legal representation," totally evading my request. I asked several times, and she would not share any of the information with me.

Courage Under Fire was no longer mine. I wonder today if it ever was. My entire family was outraged! They were so mad at me I wasn't even allowed to use the phone anymore! They made my life miserable because I was being forced to see the truth for what it actually was.

I knew something had to be done, but I felt like I needed Gwendolyn's assistance. She was, after all, the only person I knew willing to spend enough time and invest enough effort to aid me in completing the work. Gwendolyn Peabody, whom I knew I should be avoiding, became my closest ally. I went to the Protective Services Agency, through WACS, and established residence in a foster home. Gwendolyn had spread the word that my family had turned against "our" project. The staff at the center noticed an unusual relationship developing between the two of us.

Julie Cramer, Dr. Holder's administrative assistant after Sallie Reader left, approached me about Gwendolyn. She was concerned that things were getting out of my control. Everyone was recognizing my relationship with Gwendolyn for what it was, and in my powerlessness, things were worse than ever. Even Uncle Nora was so frustrated with my inability to handle the situation that he constantly scolded me.

Gwendolyn was no longer coming over to the house. The family was threatening her, and she was scared. Her paranoia grew to the point where she was afraid to reside in her own condominium. Julie suspected I was being taken advantage of by her, and so did Teresa Hartsfield, the replacement teacher for Pam Smith. Dr. Holder resigned as director of the WACS program around this time.

Julie is a no-nonsense type of person. She is direct, straightforward, and doesn't like shifty characters or situations. She warned me, if I wanted to move out of Momma's house I would have to stay out. She could arrange for me to be placed in a foster home. That was, however, to be a temporary arrangement. Julie felt the time had come for me to take the boldest steps of my life, establishing my own place of residence.

Teresa disagreed with Julie about the instability of my living arrangements, but not about Gwendolyn. Teresa and I talked about Momma's dedication to me. She pointed out how much I depended on Momma and viceversa. Momma had, after all, been unstinting in her love and support of me throughout my life. She had specific ideas about what someone with a disability can and cannot do. I know countless other virtuous people who underestimate the undeveloped potential contribution of disabled citizens, and therefore actively limit their opportunity, in the same fashion as Momma.

Momma was hurt and upset by all the hatred at home. She had already lost one son and would view, in Teresa's eyes, my departure as the loss of another. After some discourse between us, the choice was left up to me. I took everything into consideration.

I decided, after a break, to move back home. I would arrange with Momma to stay at home and pay rent to her directly. This would remain in effect until such time as I could find an apartment suitable for my needs. She wasn't going to like it, but that's how it had to be for the benefit of all concerned. Julie, Teresa, and I made final arrangements to put the plan into action in two days.

Now you should be getting a clearer understanding of the multifaceted relationship I had with Gwendolyn Peabody. By February of 1984 she had my trust completely and without question. Though she had entered into almost every aspect of my life, our relationship was 100 percent platonic. It didn't appear that way to some people, who theorized that we might be more than friends.

She was my advisor in all aspects of my public and personal life. She had this crazy idea that I was like Helen Keller, incapable of any comprehensible expression without her help. She liked to think of herself as my teacher, my Anne Sullivan, of sorts. She even went so far as to hang a picture of Helen Keller leaning on Dr. Sullivan's shoulder on the wall of my bedroom!

She told me how to act, dress, and speak for any and every occasion. She counseled me on the best way to treat my family, friends, and acquaintances. At times, she even told me how to deal with my love life. This guidance subtly changed over the years into control, until Gwendolyn dominated almost every aspect of my life. Unbelievable as it may seem, this was all accomplished with the power of money.

Like everyone I grew up with, I have never had money and had never been close to it at any time in my life before I met Gwendolyn Peabody. Therefore, when she told me I needed to rely on her "advice" for a situation involving anyone new or any kind of money-related experience, I trusted her judgment unconditionally. That included anything: stores, malls, grocery shopping, movies, dates, restaurants, and many other places and situations. Successful in her attempts to socially refine me, with obviously positive results, Gwendolyn's advice slowly filtered into other areas.

Put yourself in the shoes of someone who never had anything: no reliable car, no decent clothes, nothing materially valuable. Practically no one in your family has had anything as far back as you can trace your jeanalogy. I have just described my own family and most poor families. Poverty is the background I come from, one of pride and constant struggle, one of triumph, and too often of despair.

My family resented Gwendolyn deeply, and our friendship put me in a position of authority over Jean and the others. Generosity can have more than one effect on the deprived. What she spent on me made my life better. The emotional expenditure by a person of wealth on someone of my lineage and limited education also had a powerfully controlling effect upon my self-image.

It is easy, under impoverished circumstances, to be resentful of people with money. Why do rich families see their success as totally unconnected with our lives? The richest people in our country could not possibly increase and maintain their wealth without somehow hurting wages and benefits of workers in the average American family. Poor children find evidence early in life that the American Dream of liberty in coexistence with equality of opportunity is an unmitigated lie. Discovering that lie leads many underprivileged children to begin selling drugs, for example, or just about anything that will bring money directly into their lives.

Children of the ghetto grow up in a distinctly separate society, one foreign and utterly disconnected from even an awareness of our culture of "opportunity" by traditional American definitions. Ghetto kids are focused on their own literal daily survival. The scene outside their front doors is marked by evidence of the vicious economic neglect, learned violence, and hopelessness of those likewise written off before these kids were even born. This cycle of poverty is a bubble isolating their experience so completely that twelve years of public schooling becomes their first taste of a culture many cannot believe in or adapt to during an all too brief span of time. In my old neighborhood, many young people see more potential for earning tangible money in drugs than in the unbelievable value of a college degree.

My family has been rent asunder by petty lawsuits over nothing other than the fact that none of them had any money. Momma's piece of mind was destroyed by the loss of Milton's money. Gwendolyn recognized that ignorance in me of anything even remotely related to a lifestyle involving money. She also knew at that time I would have done anything and agreed to any condition which would bring money into my life or place me in a more competitive position with my friends and siblings. She exploited my weakness to the fullest.

Of course, I do not look at money this way now. It took my experience with Gwendolyn to teach me how insignificant money really is. It is a means to an end, rarely used in the most visionary ways. Money makes it possible to fulfill material dreams. A sound mind and a selfless heart, validity of purpose; these are the only real tools useful for fulfilling authentic dreams.

The Sun Shines Again

Peterson is a town about forty-five minutes away from the city of Tuscaloosa. The couple I lived with, Ted and Carol Johnson, were one of many families in the state of Alabama paid to house abused people. Monday through Friday, Carol would bathe me, dress me, and we would leave for WACS at 7:30 in the morning. During the two weeks I lived in Peterson, the Protective Services Agency did a thorough investigation into my personal and domestic affairs. They couldn't believe what they found. I was thirty years old and not aware of any of my personal rights!

When I found out I could cash my own checks and manage my own money, I was overjoyed. In my first week away from home, I went to the Social Security Office and had both monthly checks transferred over to my name. Momma had been the overseer of my money, giving me what she was advised by other family members, for the last twelve years. I established two accounts with two different regional banks. This gave me a main account and a reserve account for actual savings.

I went to the Federal Building and got my first social security card. Along with my student i.d. photo, I could use it to cash checks on my own. During the second week, I went to talk with Momma. She was very hurt and confused about the circumstances.

"Momma, we've got to talk."

"Okay, let's talk."

"I know you are hurt and disappointed in me, but I am doing this for me and for you. It's not that I don't appreciate what you've done for me, it's just time for me to pull my own weight."

"This ain't you talkin', this is dat damn Gwendolyn talkin' through you. She's the one dat has done dis."

"Gwendolyn had nothing to do with this decision of mine. I did it all on my own."

"I know, Nathan, dat you think you can do these things, but you cain't."

"I am going to do this whether you or anybody else likes it or not!"

I moved back in and tried my damnedest to work things out with the family. Momma went behind my back and had those checks transferred back into her name! I corrected the situation by having them sent to WACS, where I would receive them and go downtown to deposit them into each bank account. While Momma and I fought, the people at the Social Security Office arranged for both checks to be directly deposited into my accounts. It's been that way ever since.

The tension mounted rapidly, reaching new heights, but I stood firm. I was no longer a child, and it was time my family gave me the respect I deserved. For the first time in my life, Momma could not exercise her authority over me. I was becoming my own man, finally. At age thirty I had full control, for the first time, of my own finances.

During 1985, I worked toward becoming more independent and assertive. I was paying rent and bills, buying my own clothes, going to movies. Gwendolyn was not financially supporting me any more. In fact, between arguments, she was teaching me how to budget my money. With her help, I had fifteen hundred dollars saved and was living a comfortable lifestyle. I started standing up to Jean, putting my sister in her place.

On November 6, 1985, Annie Bell discovered my Aunt Joyce had cancer. She'd been battling cancer for many years and kept it to herself. Auntie suspected this to be true for some time, but she didn't find out for sure until Joyce came to her, asking for a ride to the doctor's office. The doctor, upon examining Joyce, was shocked to discover to what degree cancer had decimated her kidneys. He gave her some medicine for pain and sent her home, to be cared for by her sisters.

Aunt Joyce died on December 7, 1985. Being divorced, she did not leave a will, she left verbal instructions with Annie Bell and Momma, regarding her personal effects. Annie Bell has been estranged from the family since Joyce's death, over an argument about three thousand dollars Joyce told Annie Bell she had stored in the closet which turned up missing after Sheila had been in my deceased aunt's home. After the accusations flew, Momma and Annie Bell fought bitterly for ten years. If Joyce had shared the information about her secret stash with both her sisters, then the whole thing could have been avoided.

I was disgusted to the point of rage, and voiced my opinion to everyone, whether they liked it or not. "In a family like ours, why in the hell does money have to be the most important concern when someone dies?" I made up my mind to have no part of it at all. As the anger ignited on both sides, I began to seek help from the staff at WACS in looking for an apartment.

Julie Cramer had heard of an experimental program beginning soon in Birmingham called the Gerry Fullan House, and the more I learned about it, the more I realized I must be a part of it. A prototype in independent living, specifically designed for people with developmental disabilities, the Fullan House is currently funded by United Cerebral Palsy of Greater Birmingham. Three weeks after we sent in my application, I received a phone call from Gary Edwards, executive director of UCP in Birmingham. The building was scheduled to open on February 17, 1986. We set up an interview for one of the nine available slots in early January. Gary was very impressed with me, and after an hour long interview, I became part of the initial team.

The Fullan House, the first of its kind in the state, is a boot camp to teach life management skills to people with severe disabilities. Tenants are in charge of everything, from arranging their utility connections to hiring their own attendants. We would be washing our own clothes, making our own beds, cooking our own food, cleaning our own apartments, and designing our own budgets. All of this was, of course, with assistance, but it was designed to allow as much independence and freedom as possible.

The Department of Housing and Urban Development (HUD) customizes each tenant's rent, based on his or her individual income. The home is staffed by three resident house managers. The managers are responsible for upkeep of the house, food preparation, trouble-shooting, and settling domestic disputes. The Independent Living Center, a state financed referral agency and training center, also plays a critical role at the Fullan House. They are responsible for basic education, training tenants to hire their own attendants, shop for their own groceries, cook, and do a variety of other things.

Each person's stay at the Fullan House is temporary. The average tenant remains about three to five years. I realized, as I learned about the program, it would be the ideal springboard from which I could eventually land in my own apartment. It became the most exciting thing I had ever been involved with.

Let me share some details about training and activities at the Fullan House that made life so interesting. We lived not by HUD funds alone, but by the many telethons arranged by UCP of greater Birmingham. Our first telethon was in January of 1987. The Gerry Fullan House was the talk of the town, and we were considered to be the forerunners in a new and unprecedented program to prepare disabled people for the "real world." Gary Edwards presented all eight of us as success stories. We turned on the charm and the phones started ringing. Somewhere in the neighborhood of $100,000 was raised, a large portion of which went to our house.

We represented the model program for disabled education across the nation. Our "reality training" was very informative. Balancing a checkbook, cleaning and maintaining an apartment, dealing with bills and budgets, approaching an uncooperative neighbor, safety, emergency procedures, cooking, developing interpersonal relationships, and sex education were some of the topics we covered during my three years at the Gerry Fullan

House. In the next few years, other houses sprang up throughout the country. HUD inspected our house annually with scheduled and unscheduled visits. We kept on our toes, and most of the time they were unequivocally impressed. We stayed neat, clean, and organized.

Miss Gerry Fullan is a Birmingham philanthropist who donated the grounds to UCP for the building site. She has spent many years of her life working with cerebral palsy individuals. Everyone who experiences life there has Miss Fullan to thank. Money comes in from various UCP functions and private donations throughout the year. Rabbi Milton Grafman, of Temple Emanuel, for example, was responsible for raising around $34,000 at a humanitarian award dinner during my first year.

The first open house at our place of residence caused a media frenzy! On June 20, 1987, we would open our doors to a variety of health professionals, congressmen, news reporters, local politicians, and a host of others. I was asked by Gary and Charles Priest, our administrator, to prepare an informative speech describing our daily activities and long-term goals. The event went off without a hitch, and everyone who came was inspired by what they found. We found worth in the optimistic concept of Gerry Fullan, and it remains worthy today.

There are now three houses in the Birmingham area. With available HUD funds, the newest two opened in 1993. They are smaller, and better equipped than the Fullan House, but all three are vital to the lives of Alabama's disabled community. Gary is lucky to have significantly more available resources than other UCP regions in the state of Alabama. I would like to see several more houses similar in design open soon. It is probably surprising to learn, but Alabama is actually one of the pioneering states in the country, where laws affecting the disabled community have become a priority in the last ten years.

I would like to open a home in Tuscaloosa similar to the Fullan House concept, but with a few modifications. I would overestimate each resident's potential, the precise opposite of the approach taken today. Assistive technology and devices would be continually updated, and the estimated costs of this would be taken into account when the annual budget is determined. I would design it with the goal in mind of maintaining a state-of-the-art program, the way it was for me.

The Fullan House remains an important stepping stone toward independence for a disabled individual, along with the RISE concept and WACS at the University of Alabama. I moved out of my house in Northport and stayed three weeks in a group home before the big day arrived. Julie and Teresa acquired a disabled-equipped University of Alabama van, and carried me to my new Birmingham home. I never had the chance to meet any of my neighbors beforehand and really didn't care. I always love meeting new people, and expected the unexpected.

Mike Holsmbeck, Ronnie Eustis, and I were the first three to arrive. Lisa Owens, Ray Bledsoe, Kim Mitchell, Phyllis Weeks, and Randy Pruitt moved in throughout the day. Our ninth member, Buster, came in that day and left that night, never to be seen again. He was replaced by a guy named Tom. The house managers had all been hired, but the amount of dedication the job requires was too much for one, and she quit in the first week. The two remaining were Rachel Smith and a lady named Rhonda. Our replacement manager was Connie-Lee Swope. One of my many mothers, she is Senior Staff Member at the Fullan House today.

In the first three months my world changed dramatically. I went from nearly total dependency to virtual autonomy, at least in a communal sense. Coming from various backgrounds, discovering our equal prejudices, similar fears, goals, and needs, we forged a difficult, though successful, community. For example, I have a distaste for rednecks like Ray Bledsoe, and he had an equal aversion to living with blacks. I realized the more we relied on each other, putting aside racial issues for a common goal, the more independent we became.

The most important thing we realized was the value of each other. No one else knew better how to tend to our needs than ourselves, so Ray and I learned to respect each other. We shared information and utilized our collective strength to ensure everyone was learning the same things at the same time. Coming out of a nursing home, Mike had more experience than I in hiring attendants. I had more public relations experience than anyone else and educated the group in self-expression. We formed a family that fit together like clockwork, offering assistance to each other whenever necessary.

Connie Lee-Swope has had an important role in each person's development. Of the many incredible people I have ever known, she ranks in the top five. From the first day of her appearance on the scene, Connie accepted the arduous role of den mother/drill sergeant of the house. Her limitless patience and undying devotion to both the tentants and ideals of the Fullan House are exemplified in the amount of time, far exceeding what she is paid for, that Connie spends on each individual's needs. Many who pass through those doors owe Connie an indeterminable debt for the role she plays in reshaping their lives to feel and believe themselves to be independent.

Between the years of 1984 and 1987, my life was a roller coaster ride of turmoil and discovery. The book project was falling apart, but mixed in with the nonsense was a vigorous determination to make a better life for myself. I said I would never move back in with Momma, but that does not imply that I was not welcome. Whatever happens, I will always have a home in Northport. Momma kept all the required equipment to take responsibility for me, but it will not be used again. I take responsibility for myself now.

A Moving Experience

It was the beginning of my stay at the Gerry Fullan House, and I was still healing from a bad departure in Tuscaloosa. I'd just had the worst experience since my suicide attempt. Telling my family I was moving out of the house and starting over, in Birmingham, created unprecedented turmoil. Auntie and Uncle Nora were the only two I could turn to for comfort and support.

I had been there three months, from February seventeenth to April eighth. I will never forget that April morning as long as I live. At 10:00 a.m., I was in the office using the phone when a knock came on the front door. A nameless wonder arrived, asking to speak with someone about an attendant job. She wore a white sundress, patterned with sky blue polka dots. As she timidly stepped through the doorway, I was awestruck by her magical beauty.

I said, "If you will follow me, I will get someone for you immediately." I asked for her name. She timidly replied, "Mary." And she smiled. It seemed like . . . God, when she smiled, a calming effect came over me. I felt like something was telling me this was the one who would help me overcome the pain I had endured for so long. Leaving her in the office, I went to get Connie, who was too busy to turn loose from what she was doing, and she asked me to handle it.

Upon my return, I reached into the file cabinet and found Mary an application. She asked my name, and I told her, "Nathan." I saw a distinct glimmer in her eyes and knew that something undeniable was developing between us. As she filled out the application, I studied her form intensely, from head to toe.

She asked me, "Is there anything wrong?"

"No. No, there isn't anything wrong," I replied. She turned back to her half-completed application. In a moment of serenity, God put something special together between two needing individuals. Just by her appearance, I could discern many similarities between her life and my own. Mary was a survivor. She had overcome many obstacles and was determined to rise above her circumstances in the most expedient way.

Completing the paperwork, she laid down the pen and turned to give it to me. For the first time our eyes met, and an explosion of emotion passed between us. In those rich brown eyes, time and space lost their meaning. The journey we would embark upon would be turbulent and dangerous, involving genuine passion, unrealistic dreams, and ultimate betrayal. Here begins the love story of Nathan Ballard and Mary Dates.

Seeing my utter disregard for what she had placed into my hand, Mary inquired, "Why are you looking at me, Nathan?"

I replied, "I have to admit; there is something wrong. You have affected me in such a way that I can't stand it."

She said, "I feel the same way, Nathan." Then she whispered to me, "I must have this job. Put in a good word for me."

I promised from the bottom of my heart, "Mary, I will do my best. Stay here and don't move. Don't go anywhere until I come back." I went to talk with Connie and Mike. I explained the situation to them both, but discussed things with Mike, "I have an applicant here for the attendant job." As he glanced over the application, I continued, "Mike, let's give her an interview."

"Okay, Nathan," he assured me, "We'll interview her later this afternoon. Can you ask her to come back around three o'clock?" I agreed to his arrangements and hurried back around front. Mary was sitting on pins and needles, and I knew it.

"Can you come back around three o'clock this afternoon?"

"God knows, yes, I can, Nathan. Yes, I can. God knows I can!"

"Well, I've done my best. I think you got the job."

Down in my guts, I was determined to get her this job. She needed this place as badly as it needed her, as badly as I needed her. Mary knew I was wholehearted. She stood up and took my hand, "I thank you, Nathan, from the bottom of my heart. I thank God for you." The hurt and pain of my past left me for an instant, as I immersed myself again in her eyes. Our spirits became intertwined in a rainbow stretching to the ends of the earth. She walked out the door looking at me over her shoulder. When that eye contact was broken, a part of me left with her.

As I went back to my room, I passed Connie. One look at me, and she knew something profound had just occurred. She followed me back to my room, and respectfully asked, "Nathan, is everything all right, son?"

"Yes. Everything is all right now, Connie."

"Do you want to tell me about it?"

"No. Not right now, Connie, but I will later."

As the hours passed I could do nothing but think about Mary. I asked silently, "Why now, God, did you bring her to this house? Where will I find the courage to ask her out? I hardly know this girl, but I think I love her. The question is, does she feel the same about me? Make her mine, God. Make her mine." I sat pondering until Connie knocked on the door. She was very concerned and wanted to have a long talk with me after lunch.

We went together into the living room. After our meal, Connie and I sat and talked for about an hour. I explained to her that hiring this girl was incredibly important. She could help me a great deal. I told Connie about my pain and abuse. The loneliness I felt in Tuscaloosa was a result of many things, and I explained the kindred feeling I had to Mary. Connie understood everything.

"I know you've been hurt bad, but how bad I don't know yet."

"Yes, I have, worse than you realize."

"I can tell, Nathan."

"Connie, there are people in Tuscaloosa I feel obligated to. I have let them down."

"You don't owe nothing to nobody in Tuscaloosa!"

When our conversation ended, I went back to my room and cried for a few minutes. I thought about what she said. Connie had a good point. Momma had only been a good mother. As far as my promise to Dr. Mathews was concerned, I would finish my college education when I was better equipped to do so. Now was not the time, and what about Gwendolyn?

Jim was exasperated to the point where he was about to completely give up on the project. Gwendolyn would never know how close he was to trashing it. I could care less about *Courage Under Fire*, one way or another. This was my sabbatical, the chance to get my priorities straight again. Connie reminded me that my priorities should begin with me.

The pleasant faded blue of my room's flowered couch was all the more evident in sunlight entering from the opposite window. The sun caught dust particles in the room and a resulting beam warmed my upper body. I contemplated for about thirty minutes, my mind adrift, entertaining thoughts of the past, present, and uncertain future. Then I saw her coming, ten minutes before her scheduled meeting. "She's even early. All the better," I thought, as she locked the door to her maroon striped, white 1976 Ford Fairlane and came toward the door.

Opening the door, I said, "Mary, won't you please come in? It's good to see you again." I led her to a cluster of rooms, unoccupied and located in the back of the house. We chose a room and waited for Connie and Mike. After their arrival, and some brief small talk, we began the interview.

Choosing a suitable attendant is a meticulous task, to be approached with the highest degree of thought and careful consideration. Disabled people must rely on their attendants, to complement individual weaknesses with necessary strengths, for whatever is required in the daily routine. An ideal attendant is responsible, trustworthy, diligent, and somewhat mechanically oriented. The most reasonable thing expected from a good attendant, however, is prompt attention to duty. They must arrive as scheduled, be it morning, afternoon, or evening.

Say you have cerebral palsy. At eight o'clock in the morning, you have an appointment with the dentist. I don't know how it is where you live, but in Tuscaloosa such appointments must be made a month or more in advance. If your attendant does not appear with enough time to get you up, bathed, dressed, toileted, and basically ready for the day, you'll miss your appointment. Punctuality is crucial in a health care attendant. This is what we impressed on Mary.

Mary, it turns out, had training as a health professional. Our attendants with her training are rarely found unemployed, and we were excited to have her with us. She was hired, and I was relieved. She would work two days a week at first, as the weekend attendant on staff. Extra hours might come, on an as-needed basis, during the week. This arrangement was much to her satisfaction.

The work was very satisfying to her. It is truly something to work with the disabled. The spiritual quality of the work is frequently overpowering. It can also be highly physically demanding. Mary thrived on the whole experience. As she became familiar with us, the work became easier. Mary brought many innovative ideas to the Fullan House and helped to stylize attendant care. The transfer techniques she modified for her small frame are useful today for attendants working at the Fullan House who aren't as strong as others.

She and I worked as a team. Mary helped everyone realize that, in order to get the best service from our attendants, we should cooperate by offering any advice or assistance we could. This is the best way. It's how I train my attendants today. Just like with everything else, respect is the key: respect your attendants and they will do the same.

It's very important to never place an attendant in a spot where they have no control. Whenever possible, give them ample time and warning when assistance is mandatory. This will avoid embarrassing situations for you both. And always do everything on your own, requesting assistance only when it becomes an absolute necessity. Independence is a minute-to-minute battle. Don't sacrifice your independence at any time or in any way. Last, but vital: Pay your attendants for the job they do. Never be late or short in payment. They work hard and deserve their pay as arranged. This encourages a healthy work environment for all concerned.

Mary and I grew as friends. We would talk intimately for hours at a time. She has a terrific sense of humor, and it wasn't long before she introduced me to her family. At the time we met, her sister Betty was pursuing a degree in business at the University of Alabama at Birmingham on the other side of town from the Fullan House. Between two boys and a girl, Mary has her hands full. She has three children by two different men, not uncommon in poor neighborhoods among women who will do virtually anything to have something precious and beautiful. Her youngest, Jonel, was three years old then. Nicole was a pretty little ten year old, and Edwin, her bright-eyed eldest son, was fourteen. She had divorced her violent husband several years previously, and now had three mouths to feed, with bills to pay as well. My respect for Mary Dates grew stronger every day.

She maintained her composure for five months, working well under exceedingly stressful conditions, but began to have trouble. The stress of managing her family situation and keeping the rigorous schedule required at the Fullan House was wearing Mary down over time. She began to arrive late for work. This trend continued until a serious problem developed. Most everyone liked Mary, but tardiness in an attendant cannot be tolerated under any circumstances. I warned her several times, and she tried to keep the pace, but eight of us at once was too much for her to handle. With great pain, we fired her in October.

Out of my own pocket, I hired her back as my weekend attendant after two weeks of rest. This arrangement worked for about three months, during which I tried to convince her of the importance of punctuality. We argued about this many times, but she lost interest in the work. After releasing her from my employment, I helped Mary out with the kids as much as I could. We remained close, and she looked far enough beyond my disability to fall in love.

It happened on the third Saturday in October, the very week Mary lost her job as our Fullan House attendant. She came by the house to talk about our friendship, and we got into a deep discussion about our pasts, love affairs, private tragedies, and that kind of thing. I was in the middle of describing my rape, when she told me something that put our relationship in a wholly different light.

"Nathan, I know that you are a special person to me, but I feel sorry for you."

"Why?"

"Because I have worked around people like you before, and I just feel sorry for people in your condition."

"That's not unusual to hear. It's a part of life for those who are disabled like myself, having to deal with everyone constantly showering us with pity or looking out for what they believe is in our best interests."

"Can I tell you a story that happened to me?"

"Yes. Go ahead."

"When I was married, my husband was very abusive to me. He would come in and choke me, slamming my head up against the wall, beating me half to death. But I still loved him, despite the beatings and abuse. One day, he came in and kicked me to the floor. My self-esteem was so low, and I suffered through so much pain . . . I never knew kindness, Nathan Ballard, until you entered my life."

What could I say to that? The lines of pain were visible on her face, reminding me of the devastation in my own life. I sat and thought deeply and carefully before responding.

"Mary, no one is ever going to hurt you again, because I love you, girl."

She looked at me with tears rolling down her cheeks and said in a quivering voice, "I love you, too. No one has treated me like you. What can I do to repay you?"

"Just be Mary and always keep that smile on your face."

"I've got something that I want to give you. I can't give it to you now. I'll give it to you the night when I come back."

I knew what it was she was going to give me, or rather take from me. I think you do, too. We sat in my room, embracing each other for a while, and then she left. In the interest of her privacy, I will leave out the details, but the next Saturday night was very special, almost sacred, for both of us. Mary took my virginity that night, and at thirty-five years old, I freely gave it!

Mary helped me establish an account in Birmingham for my savings. We had to open a joint account because Central Bank of the South refused me a standard account, based on my poor writing skills. As our relationship developed, a romance blossomed. She took my flirtations in stride and became my friend. We shopped, dated, ate, laughed, cried, and had a lot of fun over the following months. We became inseparable.

An Uncertain Future

One Sunday in November, I decided the time had come to share my thoughts with Connie about the future. Mary had introduced me to some aspects of maturity. Thanks to Project Lifestlyes, and the lessons in independent living I gained under our patient coordinator, Amy Gilchrist, I felt ready to become my own man in every respect. The time had come for me to get my own apartment. When Connie came on duty that night, I called her aside and sought advice.

"I need you to tell me the truth, Connie. I am thinking about moving into my own apartment somewhere in Birmingham."

"That's good, Nathan. That's real good. Get with Amy and talk with her, but as far as I'm concerned, you are nearly ready. Almost, but not quite. You still have to get a few things through your lovably thick skull."

"I'm ready."

"I will help you all I can and share everything I know about keeping an apartment. You have to learn some things you don't want to admit. If I share my knowledge, you must listen carefully. Work with us, and we will make this as quick as we can. Deal?"

"Okay. When do we start?"

"Talk with Amy first. She will decide what direction to take. Then we'll start."

The next morning, I arranged a meeting with Amy. She set up an appointment with me for the following Wednesday. I could hardly wait. The vision burned in my mind! I pictured myself alone, self-supporting, and fully independent. Dream a little dream. It seemed like a month before I got the verdict.

"Nathan, you are at that point where you should begin to think about an apartment, but you are still lacking ability in some areas, like grocery shopping. Nathan, you haven't any experience shopping alone. What kinds of things to buy. How to recognize the best deals. Basically, you need to learn how to comparison shop. Also, you have yet to master hiring attendants. You haven't learned to be assertive when you need to be."

"I can accept that. What else?"

"Cleaning and maintaining your apartment is more difficult than you realize. What will you do if your toilet overflows? What if your sink gets clogged? How do you put out a grease fire? What do you look for in a lease agreement? What types of furniture will you buy? How will you decorate to best suit your needs? Will you work, or go to school? Nathan, these are the kinds of things you are going to have to know. Tom is also almost ready to move out. It's time we cover these issues."

This was the beginning of the end of my stay at the Fullan House. Amy, Connie, and the rest of the staff redoubled their efforts to ready us all for our eventual departure. Gwendolyn, meticulously editing "our" book in Tuscaloosa, was very excited to hear of my plans to move into an apartment. She offered to help me out as much as possible. Mary was very supportive. I even received a new electric wheelchair in February of 1988.

Jim, Gwendolyn, and I were working very closely to piece together some sort of manuscript out of the jumbled mess. We were close to a compromised version everyone would tolerate. Jim began making arrangements for actual publication in the spring. He had found a typesetter, started some pre-publication publicity, and investigated international endorsements. We even had a meeting with Gary Edwards to discuss what implications this book held for UCP and other disabled advocacy organizations, all across the country.

As fate would have it, something went amiss. Gwendolyn did not think we were ready for publication. Despite her many unwarranted suggestions, she had been a minor player in the final editing process. Jim and I had worked for several weeks, with her input, to come up with a publishable manuscript. Gwendolyn remained unsatisfied.

She claimed Jim's work was "inadequate." After all this time, she couldn't let bygones be bygones, blaming Jim for conspiring against her and destroying her work. I thought the whole situation to be ridiculous, especially since we were so close! I'd made a lot of promises to Mary and others. On March 18, 1988, Gwendolyn came to visit the Fullan House, and I decided it was long past time to settle this exasperating situation.

"Why can't you and Jim come to some type of agreement, Gwendolyn?"

"Jim does not understand me, Nathan! I am doing the best I can! Even you don't understand me."

"I understand you better than you pretend, Gwendolyn. How can you say that, after all this time?"

"All you do is spend all your time now with Mary."

"Leave Mary out of this. She has nothing to with this!"

"Yes, she does. I have repeatedly warned you to end your relationship with Mary. Mary will hurt you, just like everybody else has hurt you."

"Gwendolyn, you have just gone a little bit too far. Listen to me and listen damn good. Mary is the best damn thing that's happened to me since I left Tuscaloosa. If you still want to remain my friend, you keep Mary's name off your tongue!"

"I'm only looking out for your best interests. Mary, in relation to the book, is our biggest problem. Why does she call and interrupt us when we are working on the book, Nathan?"

"Mary is going through a lot of emotional problems now, and I mean to be there for her. If you can't understand that, you can damn leave and never come back!"

"After all I've done for you, I feel that you are abandoning me."

"I'm not abandoning you, you've just got to realize that I've got a life of my own now, and my life is going to be with people. Not just you."

Jim worked patiently with Gwendolyn and me, trying to get her to look at the book as a story and not as a dissertation. I thought we had filed for copyright. The certificate had been due to appear in my mailbox for months. Jim and I, on the assurance from Gwendolyn it had been mailed, called the Library of Congress to verify their receipt of the forms. It turns out my esteemed partner mailed them in, all right. She merely made some slight revisions in the paperwork. Revisions we never thought to ask about, I might add, that even the Library of Congress would not accept, at first.

By now, Gwendolyn was planning a use for the book I was not even made aware of. We'll get to that later. She was actively trying to end my relationship with Mary, by doing strange things. She even took an $89 dress I bought for Mary because it wasn't bought for her. She was controlling me through my own book. I needed an apartment, with my own keys, and the sooner the better.

In April, a new neighbor moved in named Gordon Richmond, replacing Randy, and he immediately struck me as some kind of genius. Gordon's severe speech impediment, due to his specific type of cerebral palsy, made it difficult for him to communicate, but the boy was sharp. He had graduated from the University of Alabama at Huntsville, not long before his arrival at the Fullan House, and had plans to utilize his abilities in accounting and economics. Gordon already possessed many of the skills necessary to survive independently, but he had not yet learned a practical way to communicate. He spent his time learning to use a speaking board.

We fine-tuned our skills, by going on outings to various places around town. Phyllis and I used to go to the movies together in our electric chairs. The specially-equipped disabled van was at our disposal. We would go into town any day of the week we wanted. This encouraged us to do as much for ourselves as we could. I remember one really funny event occurring in August, involving Phyllis, myself, and some dumbfounded store clerks.

Phyllis and I rolled into the Family Dollar Store's open door and were looking around. We noticed the suspicious reaction of the clerks, who were cautiously watching us, like we were about to rip something off. Actually, Phyllis was looking at some earrings. I understand their surprise, watching two black, severely disabled people on the town alone. Regardless, they treated us like a couple of crippled hoods.

When they found out that we could talk, those clerks nearly fell over in astonishment. They were doubly shocked to find the crippled couple had money and intended to make a purchase! With dazed stares, and glassy eyes, they rang up her earrings, and gawked at us as we approached the door. Undaunted, Phyllis exclaimed, "After you, Nathan."

I retorted, "No, no. My dear Phyllis, after you!" I held the door, as she exited, and followed her outside, where we nearly fell over laughing at their stupidity. I don't know why some people automatically associate disability with criminal activity, but they still do today. I guess it's just uneducated ignorance, but there is no excuse for it whatsoever.

Most of the time, we had a lot of fun. Phyllis was quite a woman. We worked together for ten years. She successfully moved out of the Fullan House and into her own Birminham apartment in July 1987. Her quick wit and sharp tongue made for interesting debates in Montgomery the past few years.

By early October of 1986, the only thing keeping me from getting an apartment was the hiring of a reliable attendant. I even had picked my place of residence, Birmingham Towers, located in northern Birmingham. I went through five applications and interviews before I found the right person, a lady by the name of Rowena Rhodes. Now, I was ready to move, but it wasn't a happy occasion.

Gwendolyn Peabody had effectively put a damper on the publication of the book with her stubborn attitude toward Jim's advice. She and I argued and bickered continuously about how things should be done. She hired a lady to type the book up. We agreed to split the cost of the typing. When I asked to see the invoice so I could pay my half, she told me, "Don't worry about it. I'll take care of this. Worry about getting into your apartment." When I questioned her judgment, she became agitated and squirmish.

The weeks went on. Periodically, I would ask about the typing, each time with the same answer, "It's nothing for you to worry about. I have everything under control." I believe it was probably during this time she created her book. I mean, a third-person version of the original, to be published by her, as the sole author! Her third-person manuscript, I later discovered, was meant to be accompanied by a detailed glossary of technical terms.

It seems logical to conclude she planned all along to use my book as her doctoral thesis without my knowledge, consent, or input of any kind. Why she kept it from me is beyond me. Maybe she felt I was not capable of comprehending such noble pursuits, but of course this is not true. The irony of it all was, had she even bothered to ask, I would have let her gain credit for anything that would help further her education.

In the meantime, she caused delay after delay, and kept me believing that everything would be resolved soon and my book would be on the shelves in stores. I had promised Mary many things—a new car, a marriage, and, basically, a life without financial strain. She began to question the validity of these stories, and I would always reassure her. After three months of filling her head with stories of unbelievable wealth, Mary was ready to call it quits. I can't blame her one bit.

Three weeks before I moved out, we had a huge argument. Both of us said a few things we didn't mean, and that was it. Now I had a home of my own, but I had lost Mary Dates. Before we split up, I told her, "If you ever need me, I will be there. Whatever you think, I never lied to you, and someday I will do everything in my power to make those promises come true."

Owe No Man Nothing

My first apartment was in a complex called Birmingham Towers. Gwendolyn had filled the place with a standard double bed, a used chest of drawers, four old end tables, a dilapidated coffee table, and four brass lamps. The cabinets were stocked with various used dishes, silverware, and cups, while the counters were supplied with hand-me-down kitchen appliances, like a toaster oven and blender. She had stuffed the closets with blankets, sheets, pillowcases, towels, even some new clothes. It was adequate, and in the bathroom I had every necessity.

This was jeanrous. She gave me more than I could ever have asked for, than I would ever need, and made additional promises. Pictures, posters, and other decorations were coming later. I couldn't thank her enough. I have a feeling, though, she did all of this with calculated intentions.

I suppose she figured, correctly, I would feel undeservedly indebted to her, and would then do whatever she asked in return. Gwendolyn came down the next day with pneumonia and was sick for a month. All of the commotion from the past weeks caught up with her a day after she brought down the furniture. I didn't get to thank her personally for six weeks. The first day I saw her we went poster shopping at a local mall, right before Thanksgiving of 1988.

I went home for Thanksgiving. Momma and I were trying to make peace. This trip was the trial, for everyone. In Northport I felt out of place. The atmosphere was distant. Auntie and Momma weren't speaking. Only Uncle Nora remained unchanged, but the Jacksons missed Thanksgiving dinner. The happy occasion, as I remembered it, would never be the same again. The entire next day, I visited with Auntie and Uncle.

"Nate, something is troubling you. What is it?"

"Uncle Nora, I want to get your advice on something that is very important to me."

"Son, I'll do my best to answer yo' question, but let me ask, is it a girl?"

"How did you know?"

"I have only seen dat sparkle in your eye, Nathan, jus' once before. Dat was when you first started college."

"There is a girl I met in Birmingham that I'm crazy about, and I'm afraid I'm gonna lose her."

"What've you done, Nathan?"

"Uncle Nora, I have made this girl so many promises, of marriage, of wealth, and of a life that I may not be able to fulfill."

"The promises are wit' dis book. You know, Nathan, I've always tried to be honest wit' you, in everything I've tried to tell you. I'm not goin' to start compromisin' now.

"It's like this. The world ain't gonna meet chou half way. Whatever you want outta dis world, you gots to take it because you see, son, life is give and take. You've given enough. Now it's time to take a little bit for yo'self.

"I'm an old man. I've seen a lot and I've done everythin' I've ever dreamed. If you love dis girl like you say you do, Nathan, you won't let nobody come between somp'n you start. Finish what you started."

I left Tuscaloosa on Sunday with renewed hope for the future. I felt more independent than ever before. My experience with Rowena was growing. Ours was a strictly business relationship. She would come each morning at seven and was never late. Rowena had my schedule down.

She knew what to do, and I gave her full run of the apartment: cooking, cleaning, and various other things. Rowena had even gone as far as arranging everything so I could live with the most minimal difficulty. Major appliances were now within reach of my unruly right arm. Thanks to her conscientious work, on Gwendolyn's next visit, the first I'd seen of her since our shopping excursion, my apartment was completely rearranged to my advantage, and immaculate!

"Nathan, the apartment looks real good."

"It should. Rowena has done an excellent job."

"I see you've done some changing around in the kitchen."

"Rowena did it. She made it easier for me to get things."

"But I liked it the way it was."

"Well, I like it the way Rowena's got it, Gwendolyn."

"But, Nathan, I like it the way I had it."

"You don't live here. I do. I've got to make things convenient for me."

"But it will be convenient for you the way I had it. Don't you like the way I fix things up for you?"

"Yes . . . you've been generous . . . more so than necessary."

"If you like the way I fixed things up, why did you allow her to change it?"

"Gwendolyn, you're not up here with me all the time, and things get moved around. Rowena has arranged things to make it easier for me."

"But, Nathan . . ."

There was no point in arguing. Gwendolyn wanted things her way, or no way. She immediately rearranged the kitchen. Of course, Rowena put things back in order, but every time Gwendolyn came to my apartment, without fail, she changed everything to what she thought was best for me. I grew tired of this ridiculous behavior. I put a stop to it on her fourth visit. Rowena was in the kitchen fixing breakfast for me when Gwendolyn came in, without knocking first, I might add.

"How are you, Nathan?"

"I'm fine, Gwendolyn."

"I see you've changed things back around."

"Yes, that's right, I did let Rowena change things back around."

"Now you know, Nathan, that things are going to be difficult for you the way you've got them."

"This is the way I want it, and this is the way it's gonna be!"

"But, Nathan, I'm only trying to help you. Don't you want my help anymore? You're just trying to make me feel guilty."

"I know what to do when it comes to my own attendants, Gwendolyn. Rowena is with me more than you are, and she knows what I need before I need it. Not you or anyone else is gonna tell me what to do in my own apartment! I'm not gonna allow you to continue coming in here and taking over. You will not tell me or my attendants how to take care of me, when I know damn well how to take care of myself!"

She stopped there, rushing over to the window, exclaiming, "You do not understand me." At that point, I just looked at her, unbelievingly. This was another classic case of Gwendolyn Peabody exercising unnecessary control over my life. Luckily, I did not see her enough for these predictable habits to become too bothersome.

A variety of people coexist in the unique structure that is Birmingham Towers. All twelve floors are filled with adventure. The building is shaped like one side of a medieval castle. It has two high towers with a connecting wall between them. Residents live on both sides of the hallways, on every floor, with additional apartments on each end. Some of the most bizarre, interesting, wise, sad, hilarious, lonely, and friendly people I have ever known make up the collage of residents living together in that elaborate labyrinth.

Birmingham Towers receives a majority of its funding from federal subsidies. Unlike Clara Verner Tower, my next apartment building receiving federal funding, they are not biased and racist in their housing practices at Birmingham Towers. They house a number of minority groups and actually do have several disabled-accessible apartments modified to meet the needs of someone in a wheelchair.

I lived on the first floor of Birmingham Towers, room 113. It was always busy, with people coming in and out. I spent several of my first days sitting in the lobby and wondering, "What in the hell am I doing here?" A disabled man who looked to be in his mid-forties, named Jimmie McSwain, introduced himself to me and we struck up a conversation. Jimmie received a spinal cord injury in a car wreck on May 29, 1967. He was forever paralyzed from the waist down.

I found he had a competitive spirit, much like Peter's. Over the course of a year we engaged in a fierce competition, betting big money on everything from football games to which lobby elevator would open first. Now, Jimmie had a reputation for being a ladies' man, but I soon put those rumors to rest. No man has ever been more charming than I am. Ask around.

Here's an example of a typical day at Birmingham Towers, and of Jimmie's gullibility. This happened right before Christmas of 1988:

I had purchased a worthless piece of junk jewelry from some street vendor for about five dollars, and the piece looked very genuine. What a perfect opportunity to scam Jimmie, who claimed to be an expert on jewelry. I thought the time had come to put his expertise to the test. Riding up the elevator to his seventh-floor apartment, a fiendish scheme formed in my head.

"Hmmm . . . eighteen carat gold sounds believable . . . twenty-four would be too soft." Leaving the elevator and passing through the massive double doors, turning left down the hallway, I snickered to myself. Knocking on the door to number 713, visions of dollar amounts raced through my head, his dollar amounts. Now, when did he get paid last?

"Jimmie, may I come in?"

"Yeah, come on inside!"

"What are you doing?"

"I am fixing to partake in a good cold beer. Care to join me?"

"No, man, I'll pass."

"What've you got there that is so shiny?"

"This old thing?"

"May I see it?"

"No, you may not."

"Let me see it, Nathan . . . This looks rather expensive."

"Be very careful with it."

It wasn't long before I had him convinced of the amount it was worth. I never priced it for him. He thought for sure he had got the best of me. When he quoted a value of fifty dollars, thinking seventy-five to one hundred as he eased it from my grip, the boy thought he had me.

I could probably have gotten more, but I figured fifty dollars in the hole was enough damage. A week later he showed up on my doorstep, looking a bit perturbed, with a curious green stain around his neck. Unfortunately, I was unable to refund his money but was perfectly capable of laughing my head off. What a dope!

After some heated deliberation on the subject, I said, "You're supposed to be the expert on jewelry, Jimmie. Not me."

"I will get you for this."

About a week later, he struck with a vengeance, taking me for about sixty-some-odd dollars on a San Diego–Dallas football game. Jimmie and I shared many good times. He lives in the same apartment today, still thinking of himself as cooler than I, but who can expect perfection from a jewelry expert of his caliber?

I made many other friends. Preachers, soldiers, janitors, schoolteachers, steelworkers, and all kinds of other professional working poor became acquainted with me and I with them over the course of my stay. I was more independent than ever before, and for the first time in my life I was completely comfortable within my own surroundings. That's not to say I wasn't lonely every once and a while, or that life was even remotely stress-free. On the whole, things were grand. I couldn't ask for much more.

Overcoming

Two days after Christmas, Mary stopped by the apartment. I hadn't seen her in about three months, but it seemed like three centuries. She looked strung out, like she'd been fighting to make it. I didn't like this at all but was really glad to see her.

"Mary, how are you doing?"

"Nathan, I am tired, very tired."

"You look it."

"Listen . . . I have something to tell you, Nathan. I want you to be the first one to hear this, before I tell anyone else. I am seeing someone else now."

"Who? But I thought we had something that would last."

"I couldn't tolerate the lies, Nathan. If it hurts you, I'm sorry."

"I hope he treats you good."

"I want to bring him by, so you can meet him."

"I don't want to meet him. I don't want to have anything else to do with your personal life. Leave this apartment, please."

How could I tell her? There was no way to explain. Everything I promised her was dreams, just delayed. I wish I could have provided for her, but I am poor. She had been looking down at the floor some three minutes when she sighed deeply, saying, "I can't wait for you forever."

"Mary, get out. Just get out. Go."

"You don't want me to go. I know you don't want me to go."

She came over to my chair and bent down until she had my eyes. Staring dead into my soul, she whispered, "You will always love me, Nathan. I know this."

"Oh, really? Get out of my apartment. Go! Don't you ever come back!"

"I'm not going anywhere. I'm going nowhere!"

Since she would not leave, and I was on the verge of tears, I left. I went out to the lobby and came back in a few moments. The apartment was empty. I couldn't believe what had just taken place. My pride chased away the only woman I had ever truly loved.

I sat for awhile, mulling over our past. She loved me, too. If only I hadn't been so stupid as to allow my desires to blind my reason. I missed my chance . . . never had a real chance. Now, in the desperation of poverty, she was gone.

In early March of 1989, I was in the washeteria doing my laundry when Mary walked through the door with a friend of hers. We had been conversing regularly by phone. She knew I was in the market for a new attendant and suggested her friend, Louvenia Davis. I was ready to fire Rowena. Her brother had stolen a $200 watch from my apartment, and she refused to take responsibility for it. Uncertain of Rowena's ability to control her brother in the future, I thanked Mary, and told Louvenia, after an interview, I would hire her based on Mary's recommendation.

Gwendolyn, Rowena had recently informed me, allegedly bribed her to monitor my incoming phone calls, informing her of how often Mary called. She said Gwendolyn offered her fifty dollars, and she refused. Then Gwendolyn reportedly offered her up to seventy-five.

True or not, this was a very upsetting possibility, and I confronted Gwendolyn about it the next time I saw her. Once again, she denied everything, "I told you Rowena could not be trusted." Whatever. Secretly, Rowena and I had been, for many months now, going to Tuscaloosa and working with Jim to revise the manuscript one last time.

Six months would pass before Jim and I could spend enough time together to finish our work. Louvenia became my attendant on May 4, 1987, and to help her pay some way-overdue bills, I had even hired Mary back for a short time as a weekend attendant. Our relationship deteriorated rapidly, and, in June, Mary informed me of her engagement to another man. They were to be married in September, about the same time as our intended publication of the book, with or without Gwendolyn.

After firing Mary again, following a heated argument, I hired a lady named Fannie Miles as a weekend attendant. Louvenia was coming twice a day, once in the morning and once at night. She was doing virtually everything for me, from grocery shopping to feeding me. I moped around my apartment. Many days passed sitting near the window and staring out into space with the Mary Dates blues. Some days, heartbreak can take the wind right out of you.

In July, Louvenia decided to kick my ass in gear. She came in one evening, announcing her intention of quitting at night. I had been expecting too much out of her, and I knew it. She set me straight, refusing to be my maid and attendant. It had to be one or the other. She knew I was trained to care for myself and insisted I begin doing it again.

"Nathan, I'm quitting the night shift. You don't need me. Tomorrow when I come in we'll start training you to get in bed yourself."

"But . . . Louvenia, I can't do it."

"Dammit, Nathan, listen. It is about time that you learned how to utilize the skills you were taught at the Fullan House. They equipped you well enough to do it for yourself and you are going to start now."

"I just don't think it will do any good."

"That is just it, Nathan. You keep convincing yourself that nothing works for you when you won't even try. Don't you want to get your life on the move again?"

I thought about what she said, and she was quite correct. I was unmotivated, and it meant several things. All this time I believed my personal success was due to Mary's influence in my life. I had been doing more for myself than ever before, and my self-esteem had been skyrocketing. The more I considered it, the more I realized my dependency on Mary was too great. I needed to shift my train of thought from Mary to what was now important.

If I was to survive, I had to relearn how to believe in myself. Our break taught me something very important. I could survive alone. Louvenia and Fannie Miles, who had replaced Mary on the weekends after another fight, were impressing this on me and much more. It wasn't long before I realized something else. I could not only survive, I could thrive and prosper.

Louvenia and I made a pact. She would put me in bed once more, but this would be the last time either of them assisted me in doing something I was perfectly capable of doing myself. The next day, we began a rigorous training course. Louvenia and Fannie taught me, over the next year, to do virtually everything on my own. The Fullan House trained me to function and survive independently. Louvenia and Fannie showed me how to live with dignity.

Thanks to their patient work with me, I can cook with some skill. Name your cuisine. From Hawaiian Chicken to a mean pot roast with all the fixings, if you can describe it, I can prepare it. I can do things for myself now the Fullan House would never have dreamed possible. Living in Birmingham, I had a bathroom with two handrails, and enough room to get from the chair to toilet and back with limited or no supervision. I learned to get myself into bed each night, and plug up my battery charger unassisted. This kind of stuff is well beyond the expectations of any program I have ever been involved with.

My formal challenge to anyone else in my shoes is to try to top it. As far as I'm concerned, few physically challenged people do everything they are able to. For that matter, I know even more people who are not disabled in any way and still depend on others to do things for them that they are perfectly capable of doing themselves. I have one fully functional limb. What's your excuse for being unnecessarily cared for?

Mary was about to be married. My heart was torn to bits. She knew what I was feeling and offered me one last opportunity for intimacy before her wedding. I took her up on it. Mary invited me to her wedding, but I declined. She deserved better than I had to give, and I wouldn't watch her married to someone wrong for her.

Her husband, as I figured, was not the right person for her. He started smoking crack cocaine, and their relationship went to the dogs. He was unemployed and sold the few things she owned, using all their assets and savings to support his drug habits. By July of 1990, she was in a bind again, unable to work or pay her bills.

In desperation, she resorted to covert measures. On July 3, 1990, Mary went into our joint account, which remained that way even after I had left the Fullan House. She withdrew all $300 of my savings to buy groceries and pay rent. The months following Mary's marriage were troublesome for us both.

I had an accident on January 15, 1990, trying to get into bed. I jackknifed out of my chair before I could remove my right leg strap, and hung suspended by one leg strap, with my body contorted into a position where all its weight rested on that one leg. The initial strain caused me to cry out in sheer agony, but everyone outside of my apartment ignored me. I hung that way all night long, for nine hours, during which I passed out twice from the exhausting and agonizing pain.

Louvenia found me in the morning and cut the strap with a butcher knife. Then she dialed 911 (which began as a service in Haleyville, Alabama, I happen to know) and the paramedics rushed me to Carroway Hospital. No one knew how badly I had been injured. Nothing was visible, but I was in continual distress for almost nine months. In April of 1990, two days before Easter, Dr. Zeiger at Carroway Methodist Medical Center diagnosed my condition as a form of pain called "sciatica." It is relieved through various procedures. I underwent a lumbar sympathectomy to lengthen my right hamstring and tendons in an effort to relieve the damage caused to my sciatic nerve, from the knee down. The operation was a partial success, but a burning, stabbing, chronic pain has persisted, despite the best efforts of talented doctors at Carroway.

My venerable uncle became seriously ill and was hospitalized on and off during this period. The last time I saw him was in the fall of 1989. Auntie developed breast cancer, and due to the operation, she was unable to attend to his needs. She hired a man named Vermon Collins to care for him during his last months at home. Nora Lee Jackson died on July 27, 1990.

Vermon made the last days of Nora's life very comfortable. My uncle loved to smoke a good cigarette, and lung cancer is what eventually killed him. I don't smoke. I never have, nor will. Thanks partly to his teachings, unlimited and unconditional patience, wisdom, and love, I have grown into the kind of man he would have demanded. Nora valued truth. Our last conversation is as clear in my head as if it happened yesterday.

"Nathan, you and I have had a life together, son. I am very old and tired, and I am very proud of you. There is one thing I've always tried to teach you. Be true to yo'self, and always believe there is nuthin' dat you cannot accomplish in life. The only limitation that you set is yo' opinion of yo'self."

"How do you mean by that, Uncle?"

"You are livin' better now than you have lived in yo' whole life. I won't be wit' chou long. A lot'a people said dat you and I wouldn't make it, but I knew down deep we had to make it. God gives every man a choice in life. The choice is to rise up an' be something or to die as nothing. You've made yo' choice. Stick to it."

I left his hospital room knowing I would never see him again. Curiously enough, this did not make me sad. Instead, it motivated me further. I made a promise to him long ago that I would make myself into someone special. Silently, I vowed to continue on the road I started, to do my best. I had to resume my studies. I had to complete my book and get it into print, Gwendolyn or no Gwendolyn. I was not in a position to see Jim on a regular enough basis. The time had come to leave Birmingham. I had to move back to Tuscaloosa.

Momma, Sam, and my stepfather, James Douglas Welch, helped me move my things back home and into storage. It was difficult to leave Birmingham, but I had no choice. Louvenia and Fannie, who remain friends, were heartbroken when I told them the news. I said good-bye to everyone, especially Jimmie, and checked into the hospital on April 15, 1990.

I discovered Mary's theft on July 10th. The bank conducted a formal investigation and asked if I wanted to press charges. Of course I didn't. I knew Mary wouldn't have taken the money unless she was in serious trouble, and believe me, she was. Her family was close to starving, at the time.

Following my surgery, I was placed on several soporific medications that were very expensive and not covered by Medicare. Xanax, for example, costs about thirty-five dollars for fifteen pills. I went without, so her family could eat. She apologized, but I didn't care. I could go without pain medicine. Her children could not go without food.

I have done many things for Mary she has never been aware of, including paying her electric and phone bills when she thought the church was responsible. Once Jonel needed a new pair of shoes. The church didn't pay for those either. Louvenia was my instrument of good will. With her help, from July of 1990 to October of 1994, I quietly did everything in my financial power to help Mary Dates and her family.

I stayed in constant pain. With Gwendolyn's help, I went back to the UAB pain clinic on a weekly basis. My diagnosis determined I still needed something to relieve the intense and sporadic pain in my lower right leg and foot. I missed Uncle Nora's funeral because I was in such agony; I couldn't even leave Momma's house, unable to care for myself under such duress. Jim put our plans on hold until I felt like working, which would be a whole year later, after two more operations at UAB Hospital.

On November 7, 1990, I underwent exploratory surgery. Dr. Stewart Stevenson, of Russell Ambulatory Center, placed a long needle in my spinal column. The injected medicine would determine the location of the pain. If successful, it would mean I had sustained a spinal injury that was not localized in my lower right leg and foot. Dr. Stevenson's suspicions proved true. I had a spinal injury, and there is precious little that can be done to treat problems of a spinal nature. He scheduled a new and specialized operation for the twenty-sixth of December.

The morning following a very uneventful Christmas for the splintered family in Northport, Momma and Sam drove me to the UAB clinic, where I checked in to begin surgical preparations. Louvenia visited me in the hospital the afternoon before my spinal operation. Fannie called, expressing her concern. I owe them a great debt. Louvenia is one wonderful lady, and Fannie has a heart of gold.

Dr. Griffith Harsh performed the procedure, a dorsal root rhizotomy, on the sections of my spine that controlled feeling in my right leg. For the most part, it was a success. I experienced no pain for two years, and only had a reoccurrence during the writing of this book, when a friend accidentally twisted my right foot getting me out of his car. I was discharged New Year's Eve, and went back home to Momma where she could take care of me until I could regain my strength.

I started my rehabilitation at West Alabama Rehabilitation Center, thanks to Mary Williams, in February of 1991. I had to have special equipment at home to recuperate. She supplied the funds and equipment. Mary Williams is the greatest. Without her help I would never have moved into and out of Clara Verner Tower, resumed my studies, started advocacy work again in both Tuscaloosa and Montgomery, or realized my dream.

Reaching for the Sky

My rehabilitation process was long and arduous. I was easily fatigued and still recovering strength from the previous surgery. Starting in early February, each Monday, Wednesday, and Friday, I would be picked up by Tuscaloosa Metro Transit Authority and taken to Rehabilitation Services. There, a series of strenuous exercises would aid me in relearning how to sit upright and develop a full range of motion in my limbs. We began with something simple.

Since my accident, I had been unable to wear shoes. Dot Williams, my physical therapist's aide, encouraged me to try tolerating shoes again. Each day, I would lie on a platform table. Dot would stretch my legs out of their standard fetal position and hold them in place with sand bags. It was excruciating at first, but nowhere near as bad as my bracing days of old. Within two weeks, there were noticeable results. My balance was stabilizing, and I was already able to sit upright. Over time, my legs became tolerant of the pressure exerted by my weight. After a month of hard work, I was able to sit with my legs strapped to a wheelchair, and, leaning forward, I could successfully touch my toes.

The hardest thing for me to overcome was a deep-seated fear of falling out of my wheelchair again. I still am very anxious whenever one of my feet slips off its footrest. Having both feet in place is extremely important to maintaining proper balance. Going through that harrowing ordeal has taught me vigilance concerning safety procedures when I am alone in my apartment. I have occasional nightmares today, but sleeping soundly without thinking about the accident was impossible for many months. The physical therapist, Lynn Bostick, released me in May with confidence that I was well on the road to a full recovery, both physically and mentally.

West Alabama Easter Seal Rehabilitation Services continues to provide for a variety of people with orthopedic rehabilitation needs. They deal with a variety of ailments from arthritis, head injuries, and developmental disabilities, to anyone else needing physical therapy. They played a vital role in my recovery, as they have in the lives of innumerable others. Dot Williams is still on staff, and keeps tabs on my progress and whereabouts.

The family fires were rekindling. Aunt Annie Bell was a source of tension because, although I was forbidden to see her, I would go anyway. With Uncle Nora's passing, Auntie was the object of undue cruelty inflicted by various family members. She was very lonely, hurt, and misunderstood. I took it upon myself to repay all of her generosity toward me in my younger years. Momma had it out with me the first time she discovered I was seeing Auntie.

"I done tol' you not to go over dere an' see her!"

"Why not?"

"Because I said so!"

"You can't tell me not to go and see my aunt!"

"Oh, yes, hell I can, when you are livin' in my house!"

"Oh, no, you can't!"

"Since you feel dat way, you go an' live wit' her!"

That was it. I moved in with Aunt Annie Bell until I could find an apartment. I went over to Alabama Disabilities Advocacy Program, where I knew Barbara Cotter and Anne Nelson Marshall, another case advocate, would help find a way out of this predicament. They told me about Clara Verner Tower, on the University of Alabama campus. "Although a Baptist retirement community," Anne explained, "they receive federal funding, and fall under HUD jurisdiction."

I realized immediately that college was back in the picture, and graciously thanked both of them for giving me the opportunity to pursue my education again. My promise to Dr. Mathews was not in vain, after all. I was scheduled to move June 5, 1991. Until then, I lived with Auntie and helped her endure the pain she felt at the loss of my uncle and spite from the family.

Gwendolyn assisted me in getting various things for my soon-to-be new apartment and my wardrobe, holding the financial hangman's rope in her hand. I was highly suspicious of her motives. After twelve years of "working" together, my book was yet unpublished. In fact, she had in her possession the only copy. Just before my unfortunate accident, Jim and I had given our final draft over for her perusal.

When I asked her, in March of 1991, about her opinion of Jim's and my work, I made a startling discovery. Gwendolyn had fired him months ago! She never mentioned this during all the conversations after my accident. I wondered why.

It turns out Gwendolyn had gone to his home with the edited manuscript while I was in the hospital, and debated the changes we had made collectively. Jim accused her, correctly, of ruining our work together. She had gone back over our manuscript and "fixed" it back the way she had it, a jumbled and nonchronological mess, full of historical inaccuracies and misspellings. She began pacing back and forth, like she always does under stress, when Jim challenged her changes to our work.

Jim, then a man in his early seventies, became very disturbed by her appearance and manner. He threw her out, and told her never to return. I found all of this out from him when we finally spoke again in July. Gwendolyn said nothing of the problems she had getting a Library of Congress copyright. She failed to mention she had even applied for a second copyright, or that in the first she had claimed herself as sole author!

In October of 1986, as she had said, Gwendolyn sent in the copyright forms for *Courage Under Fire*, listing herself as author of the entire written text. In the second author blank she had listed me as "Subject of Book, Full Partner, Collaborator." Being the subject of my own "Biography of Nathan Ballard," as she described the nature of the text on the copyright form, does not in any way state or imply that I am the author of my own life story! The contradiction of me being "full partner, collaborator" and the book being my "biography" somehow slipped through the system and might have remained that way.

Gwendolyn is the one who inadvertently brought the issue to light when she meddled with the application yet again. Unknown to Jim or myself, effective July 7, 1990 another copyright application had been filed with the Library of Congress. It was for sole authorship of a similar manuscript with the title *Courage Under Fire*. The book was identical to the previous *Courage Under Fire*, except that it was written in third person. *Courage Under Fire #2* was complete with a prologue, epilogue, and attatched glossary.

She filled out the forms in a manner identical to her previous application four years back. This time, however, it did not go as smoothly as she had hoped. Renee C. Adams, a copyright examiner, found extreme fault with and ambiguity in her description of me. Renee wrote a letter back to Gwendolyn indicating that I must be given credit for "some text" if not as a "co-author." Gwendolyn must have anticipated the letter, catching her own mistake.

I say this because, curiously, Gwendolyn's letter back to Renee was dated as having been written several days before the copyright examiner's letter to us! Gwendolyn must have saved a drafted letter on diskette to be printed out and mailed should the authorship issue arise. In her haste to respond and clear up the mistake, she obviously forgot to change the date, making her previously drafted letter current. It was quick to apologize for the apparent misunderstanding, corecting my role in the book's development as responsible for "some text." She was now a biographer with a manuscript she had written in the third person about me, complete with a glossary of technical terms, some of her own poetry to open every chapter, and an epilogue.

A biographer writes about other people. In that alone, she incriminates herself. A "Full Partner" in the second author blank of a United States copyright application is not copyrightable; neither is "Collaborator," or, for that matter, "Subject of Book." Somehow, though, and this has confused my lawyer, Jim, and myself, her error slipped through the system the first time, in October of 1986. In July of 1990 her second application for a book with the same title, clearly changed to reflect its third-person nature, must have seemed suspicious to Renee Adams. No one among our mutual friends thought Gwendolyn capable of stealing *Courage Under Fire*, but that is exactly what happened.

Apartment 514

Gwendolyn helped me move into Clara Verner Tower, apartment 514, in early June of 1991. I was expecting the kind of accessibility that I found at Birmingham Towers, but I was dead wrong. They currently distribute a pamphlet similar to the one I read, claiming to have "twenty-four handicapped units" which are supposedly "available." Their brochure fails to mention that these apartments are designed identical to their other apartments, with the exception of one handrail in each bathroom.

What good is one handrail to someone like me? I do not even live in one of their handrail units. They promised me the "next one available," which I didn't get, not that it would make a bit of difference. I need an apartment that is accessible to my needs as someone who uses an electric wheelchair. My new apartment looked nice, but for how long?

I could tell by the width of the hallway and kitchen that it was going to be a tight fit. My walls were bound to suffer damage as a result of any attempt to maneuver my wheelchair between the bedroom, bathroom, living room, and kitchen. There is simply not enough space, and these were not the only problems I was facing. It was not as happy an occasion as my move to Birmingham. Relations between Gwendolyn and I were seriously strained, and I could tell she felt guilty about something.

"Gwendolyn, did you get the . . . uh . . . copyright back yet?"

"Nathan, don't worry about it. I've got things under control. There's no need for you to worry about anything."

She became nervous and paranoid every time I brought up the copyright issue and sought to silence me through myriad expenditures on my behalf. She bought me a new entertainment center, a used microwave, and a variety of old records and books which are in use today. I can say nothing but thank you. I knew Gwendolyn was up to something, and it was big.

She was angry with me all the time. We had been working on the book in secret from my folks for nine years, and it remained unpublished. By this time, she had totally cut me off from every decision-making process about *Courage Under Fire*. I informed her of my intentions to talk with Annie Bell about the whole situation. With a resounding "No," Gwendolyn insisted we keep everything under wraps until the publication process was complete.

I shared my concerns with Auntie a couple of weeks later, and she encouraged me to seek legal advice. Before I could do that, I needed to re-establish relations with Jim Travis. On July 3, 1991, I called him up, and we agreed to meet three days later. He had a great deal to tell me, and I him.

Jim and I realized immediately that we needed an affirmative plan of action. The next day, I went to see Richard Pryor, my case worker, and left the blue-bound, first-person version of *Courage Under Fire* in his care. I'd managed to get it back from Gwendolyn three days previously, on the promise I would return it to her when I was done reading it. Yeah, okay, sure.

Richard recommended that I talk with Don Tipper, a lawyer on staff. Don advised me, to my delight, that according to all three agreements I had with Gwendolyn, the power of attorney was in my possession. In other words, I was completely within my right if I fired her, but our financial obligation to share all proceeds from book sales remained. As far as I'm concerned, Gwendolyn Peabody had no more part in the writing of my life story from that day forward, and I suspected she had already dissolved our financial partnership by stealing the book. Now, I needed a lawyer who could prove it.

Anne Marshall told me to call a firm in Tuscaloosa that specializes in copyright matters. I left word with their switchboard operator that I needed a consultation. The man who called me back has done wonders for me. His name is Bert Guy, and I can't stress enough what a superb lawyer he is. Bert told me to finish my book with someone else. He, Jim, and I discussed this at length over the course of several weeks. The most important thing he said I should do was cut off my relationship with Gwendolyn.

I had beaten him to it already. On August 15, 1991, as far as I'm concerned, Gwendolyn Peabody and Nathan Ballard broke with each other forever. That set the task before me of finding someone willing to put forth the kind of emotional commitment that the time-consuming work of editing my book demanded. Jim and I were busy trying to fix *Courage Under Fire* for the millionth time when, on the morning of the following Thursday, August 22, 1991, I met Michael Rogers. Actually, I ran over his foot with my wheelchair.

I decided to start school again in the fall of 1991, and campus had changed dramatically in ten year's time. I registered that semester for one class, English 109, which I had to drop mid-semester. I couldn't maintain the workload without assistance similar to that available when I was involved with West Alabama Comprehensive Services. I had just come out of my English class and was headed toward the Ferguson Center, when I saw this young man reading under a nearby tree, and rolled up to introduce myself.

"Hi! I'm Nathan, and you look depressed. Do you need to talk?"

"Sure. I'm Michael, and yes. Where are you headed? I don't want to hold you up."

"Nowhere special. It is a pleasure to meet you. What is that you are reading?"

"It's called *Zen and the Art of Motorcycle Maintenance*, by Robert M. Pirsig. It's from a friend . . . about, I think, a man in search of truth through the study of rational thought."

"I am an avid reader myself. Would you let me borrow that book sometime?"

"Sure. Hey, dude, you aren't hungry by any chance?"

"Yeah, I could use a bite."

"Groovy, because I'm starved, Nathan. Let's go to lunch, my treat."

Michael and I cemented our friendship throughout the following years and found that we shared similar values. After bringing a few leftover pizzas by my apartment from the delivery place were he worked, Michael introduced me to a vibrant girl named Katy Sullivan who was born without legs. Katy graduated high school in 1997, and attends college in St. Louis. We remain buddies today.

On Wednesday, October 16, 1991, I finally met the famous Vermon Collins whom Auntie and Uncle Nora always used to brag about. Auntie recommended him as an excellent attendant after Nora's death in 1990; I had intentions of requesting him previously, but God beat me to it. I remember that day very well. My regular attendant was sick at home, and Home Health Care of North Alabama called to notify me I would be in bed until they could send someone out, around three in the afternoon.

Since I'd already missed my English class, I took the opportunity to relax and enjoy a day in bed, talking on the phone with a friend. When three o'clock rolled around, I was on the speakerphone with Annie Bell as a knock came at the door. Auntie had described Vermon Collins perfectly. As he introduced himself, I said, "You must be Vern." The look of astonishment on his face was an absolute treasure, and Auntie recognized his voice immediately.

"Hello, Vern."

"Ms. Jackson, is that you?"

"Yes, this is me, Vern. I bet you wasn't expectin' to hear from me this soon."

"No ma'am. Heh-heh . . . caught me off guard!"

"Auntie, everything you said about Vern was true. He seems like quite a comedian."

"Nathan, you are everything your aunt described and more."

Vern burst into hysterics and we hung up the phone. He spent the next hour getting me bathed and dressed, while we discussed the powerful effect of my Uncle Nora. Vern came again to get me up on Saturday and told me some more about himself.

His three boys, from oldest to youngest, are Shane, Vincent, and Brian. Brian and I share a special relationship. He is as sharp as a needle. I call him Mickey Mouse because he loves Disney cartoons. Vern, as he is known among his friends, has become one of my closest allies in the fight to get my story out.

Vern has come a great distance and will go much further in the pursuit of his dreams. Vern, Phyllis Weeks, and I graduated together in the 1993 class of Partners in Policymaking of Alabama. PIPA is an eight-month leadership training program, in becoming an effective advocate and lobbyist on the state level for disabled political agenda. Phyllis died on November 10, 1996, and her memory is continually honored by her friends.

Each year starting in 1990, the organization, in conjunction with the Governor's Planning Council on Developmental Disabilities, the Association for Retarded Citizens (ARC) of Alabama, and the Department of Mental Health and Retardation, forms a class with a maximum of thirty-five members. The number of applications each year grows at a staggering rate, but it is a selective process. The 1992–1993 class had thirty-one graduates. They were highly successful in pushing legislation through the Alabama Congress. Almost every piece of legislation we rallied behind was passed in 1993.

One of those we are particularly proud of is designed to keep people with disabilities in Alabama out of institutions and nursing homes, giving them the opportunity to have a more comfortable life. Funding has become available to families with children who require special attention. We are working on the best method of documenting individual needs and to reach as many people as possible. One such person is my friend and fellow graduate, Frances Young, whom I respect and love.

Her adopted daughter Dianne, whom I had the experience of meeting in April of 1992, is a very special young lady. Dianne has a host of disabling conditions including epilepsy, mental retardation, and some physical disabilities as well. Her experiences trying to receive an appropriate education from the state of Alabama have been less then pleasant, to say the least. Unsuccessfully trying to work with the school system in Tuscaloosa for seven years, Frances took matters into her own hands.

She joined PIPA at the recommendation of a friend and got her hands on some information concerning her daughter's rights. Then she called the Office of Civil Rights in Washington and sent them a formal complaint. Unhappily, Dianne was once kept out of a Christmas party and denied the opportunity to meet Santa Claus. Frances pulled Dianne out of Sprayberry, a school in Tuscaloosa County for disabled children, and applied for funding that would allow her child to have ten hours of home tutorial work each week. Dianne, it turns out, was attuned to home schooling. She learned more under the Lovost Program, as it is called, than she did during her entire elementary school education.

It's a very simple but effective program, designed to build a child's self-esteem while teaching a rudimentary education. This is ideal for someone like Dianne, who has had over one hundred surgeries since May of 1986 for reconstruction of her face. She needs all the love she can get. Dianne has unique needs, and requires a teacher with great compassion. Most of all, though, she needs genuine friends.

Love is appreciated in great abundance by a little girl without a face. Frances fights vigorously for her daughter's rights. In the spring of 1993, after a specially called meeting on Dianne's behalf by the Alabama Board of Education, she was successfully mainstreamed three days a week into two classes at Central High School in Tuscaloosa. Dianne is now a young adult.

Today many people are willing to work together for change, both inside and outside the system. We must understand the needs of our disabled citizens. Their diverse disabilities require articulate legislation. I, along with many professionals in the field, believe that sensitivity training is one aspect of a solution.

This is no idealistic dream. In order to fully meet their needs, it is a necessity. An active effort is currently under way to mainstream the disabled children of Tuscaloosa County. The school system is filled with individuals who agree with the idea for sensitivity training, but lack an effective means of educating faculty, students, and personnel to be more aware of each exceptional child's unique needs. I present this book as a modest building block.

My ultimate goal is to create harmony among people with disabilities and their nondisabled counterparts. All of us have shortcomings in one form or another. Together, given an opportunity to see each other's points of view, we can transform our country away from passivity and into a society where people recognize that the only mental disability is the failure to think critically and act. Some of us merely have special needs, and in my case, life in a nursing home isn't one of them.

The Americans with Disabilities Act was passed by Congress, but it needs work. With too little clarification of what constitutes a serious and significant disability, funding is a continual battle against cuts. Disabled advocates must be vigilant to ensure provisions are there until such time as the law can be amended or civic organizations can effectively replace federal programs.

In a time when we are in perilous need of more civic awareness, I find it sadly ironic that a program like AmeriCorps is under attack by the Republican leadership. Wasteful spending it is not. A program that teaches the next generation of leaders to work hard for two years before receiving the modest amount of twenty-six hundred dollars toward an education ought to be expanded at Welfare's expense. This beneficial labor teaches a lifetime's worth of lessons in the power of citizenship. From where I sit, as a board member of Civitan International, the work those kids have done in Alabama to forge ahead ADA has already been highly successful and economical.

Our AmeriCorps volunteers have options, most of which serve the disabled community. They are encouraged to choose the way they feel the most beneficial. Some construct new curb-cut and building ramps, while others assist in home care for the increasing number of severely disabled people expurgated from their former health care maintenance by budget cuts in Washington. There are many who make outstanding tutors. All of the volunteers I have met are involved for progress and growth in this country.

Money isn't the sole motivation for these kids to seek connections through two years of real citizenship. For sure, if our elected public servants in Washington reject AmeriCorps as a solution to the problem of engaging our young citizenry, they better damn well replace it with something better. Laws don't implement change, but informed people, citizens who deliberate together in an effort to create mutual awareness of all sides of an issue, do. It is high time needs of the severely and developmentally disabled were clarified, framed, and met.

I Thank God

Looking back over the course of my forty-five years, it seems as if I have lived forty-five lifetimes. So much has happened, both positive and negative, to shape my life into what it is today. The past few years have given me a more rounded perspective than I ever dreamed possible.

I have high aspirations and look toward a dream of mine called The Ballard Foundation. It would be a financial option to meet the educational needs of many future students with developmental disabilities. It would serve as a source for research funds and further dispersal of disabled housing among general student housing at state universities across Alabama first, the nation next, and then the world.

My experiences with Alabama Disabilities Advocacy Program (ADAP) have given me a deeper knowledge of what it means to advocate for people who cannot do it themselves. As a member of the advisory committee, I can effectively express needs of people with disabilities from the perspective of someone who has lived with one for over forty years. ADAP considers my input invaluable, and I accept the responsibility of the unique position in which I have placed myself.

ADAP led me to Montgomery where my experiences with PIPA have given me a deeper determination to keep fighting for what I know is right. Through PIPA I became involved with the Association of Retarded Citizens of Alabama. I served on the Aim for Excellence committee of the ARC that makes recommendations to state institutions and facilities. They try to better the living and working environment of each facility they tour in the state.

Also, I have been cochairman of the Tuscaloosa County Family and Individual Support Council. During my time of service to the organization, we met every two weeks on the Partlow campus to go over applications for financial aid. The council is unique in its format. Since it has a wide variety of services to offer, ranging from sitter services to helping a person like myself get started in an apartment, each application requires great deliberation before it comes to a vote. From 1992–94, I served a two-year appointment to the State Region II Council on Regional Family Support, that met regularly to discuss changes and more effective plans of action for reaching out to people in need.

Each organization has flaws and strengths, but at least they are here. Things of this nature were inconceivable fifteen years ago, and it is due to the hard, collective work of many individuals that they are here at all. With some 43 million disabled Americans and an estimated 846,000 Alabamians with disabilities, the requirements set down by the Americans with Disabilities Act are a definitive step in the right direction. Opinions are cheap, but organized opinions are powerful. Defending civil rights takes a lot more than just paperwork. It takes individuals like you and me and a strong will to do what is right, as opposed to what appears in the short run to be the most economical for the wealthy or largest number of registered voters.

Liberty and equality are the right of all Americans. Life in the pursuit of happiness is impossible without our society fulfilling these often expressed ideals. Equality of opportunity does not exist in this country today. I believe it remains potentially achievable. Creating an educated public requires a public more active in shaping education, crime control, and other policies that affect our lives.

With the help of people like you we can all make a difference in an often indifferent world. I have seen a lot of things happen, personally. Yet, one of the greatest things I have learned is this: If you can dream, you can always find a way to express hope. I have exemplified my thoughts, dreams, hopes, reflections, and my most intimate desires in this work. Do the same in your own.

Jim Travis, my longtime friend, editor, agent, and my would-be publisher, died of natural causes on June 13, 1994. He worked closely with me until an accident in mid-January, when he fell on the steps outside his home, leaving him unable to travel frequently. Jim's dedication, his biting wit, and undying optimism have been a source of motivation for this project through its completion. He was an eccentric man, with a giving heart and a platinum soul.

This past year has borne witness to a metamorphosis in my relationship with my mother. She has shared a great deal with me. Mom loves me dearly and has helped me understand why she says and does things in such an overly protective way. I don't think of her as mean, and she has never been unduly cruel in any way. I have made no attempt to portray her that way. Ada Mae Ballard has been a mother, looking out for what she believes to be the best interests of her son. She gives me her best. Recently, she has seen great wisdom in my ways and recognizes my independence for the first time. I can ask for no more or less.

The graduation from Howard University of my favorite niece, Nicole Danielle Clark-Brown, recently married and with child, has helped immensely in giving everyone in the family something to be proud of, especially me. I am very proud of all my brothers and sisters, nieces and nephews, aunts and uncles. I can't put into words what they have meant to me over my lifetime. Any phrase would be too trite for this family. I feel honored to be a member of the Ballard family. This book is their legacy, for our children and their posterity.

A small miracle is in the works between Mom and Annie Bell. My sister Tina got them together recently, and the family wounds are slowly mending. On December 9, 1995, Annie Bell Jackson celebrated her eightieth birthday among family and friends. She still likes to garden and attends church regularly, but is no longer able to drive around in her Cadillac. Auntie's classic car is up for sale.

In recognition of her quiet and selfless service to the community and countless people around town who in some way owe her gratitude, the city of Northport named her birthday "Annie Bell Jackson Day." This appears on the city calendar. Councilman Thomas presented her with a plaque commemorating the event. She even got a videotape to share with all the people who didn't make the ceremony.

In the fall of 1994, I felt the time had finally come to tackle college once again. I completed a New College environmental seminar taught by Ed Passerini. Assessing my needs in the classroom has helped create the criteria for a Ballard Endowed Scholarship for Severely Disabled Students, which I am in the process of funding at the University of Alabama. With the help of several friends, I have raised about twelve hundred dollars so far.

Life in Clara Verner Tower the past few years has been a sobering experience. I have made friends with a few of the residents, but many are retired Alabamians who were raised with racism and an "all-cripples-belong-in-a-nursing-home" mentality. I live in an apartment poorly suited for my needs and have repeatedly complained to the management about various conditions within it since the onset of my stay. When I tried to move to another HUD funded complex in town, my application was denied with no clear basis. I sued successfully under the Fair Housing Act and settled out of court.

Some people who work in Clara Verner Tower have always been affable and generous. Others are suspicious, accusatory, and just downright mean. I thought that while we may not like each other by virtue of our skin color, contrasting attitudes about the severely disabled, heritage, or whatever, we must all live together in dignity and associate with one another as equals. Unfortunately this has not proven to be the case. I continue to advocate for myself and work to see policies changed to better the lives and defend the rights of the disabled.

There are several reasons, including various health problems from kidney stones to a residual pain in my right leg from the accident I sustained in 1990, why it has taken me so long to finish what I started nearly two decades ago. The heart of the matter is this: One year ago I realized that I am getting older, and I've spent the last several years catching up on an adolescence I never had. After so many years of living according to other people's dictation, it has been an exquisite pleasure to explore the world at my pace and leisure for a change.

A Lesson to Be Learned

I've gleaned a serendipitous lesson from the experience of living on a university campus. This world is an exotic, fragile, and mysteriously wondrous place. I think we are, as a whole, afraid to embrace other cultures because of our inability to define, focus, and cope with our own. Everything I thought I knew about other cultures, the way they live and think, was very wrong. My opinions on things today change with the slightest shift in my information about them.

The international students I have encountered are filled with lessons, and most are eager to willingly share and listen. I met an Ethiopian student named Daniel Kebede, in 1993, who introduced me to a Japanese student named Reiko Oka. They showed me some of the world and its ethnic breadth. We have sampled each other's literature, music, art, and cuisine.

I have been studying Japanese for two years, with three other tutors since Reiko's graduation, and have mastered two of three alphabets already. I hope to visit my friends Reiko, Miho, Hiro, and Tadato in Japan one day soon. Maybe I can take some classes on Japanese culture, or assist the Japanese people in developing programs making the country more disabled accessible.

The last few years have been busy for me. I've taken time off from various responsibilities within the local disabled community, but still participate in the UCP telethons annually. I want to give the developmentally disabled a fighting chance to prove to the world that we who undergo extraordinary trials in pursuing higher education have equally unique and insightful contributions to make within the academy. No one is going to make room for us, that much is obvious.

A few years ago, I spoke with a tenth-grade English class in Tucker, Georgia. We discussed the value of higher learning. Man, were those some motivated kids! No one was more pleased than I to learn that over half the class went on to college. Now they are presented with the challenge of keeping hard work from dampening their enthusiasm. Nothing does more to break a young student's spirit than being unprepared for the discipline required to meet the rigorous demands of a diploma.

The stress of age has begun to weigh heavily on me. In June of 1995, I lost some feeling in my legs, and my kidneys had to be cleared of four large stones. I wouldn't wish that kind of pain on the devil. I am hospitalized by kidney stones every six to ten months, sometimes for two weeks and sometimes for almost two months. In between bouts with the stones, I have managed to earn an A in two Japanese language courses at the University of Alabama.

When kidney stones come, my sisters are all a boon to me. We have been settling our differences, but the process is as turbulent as peace talks in the Middle East. I guess it's evidence, though, that even the most complex conflicts have a possible solution through real communication and compromise.

Sharing is not only compassionate, it's such gratifying fun! For certain, nothing is more satisfying than shared joy. My life is a rich smorgasbord of experiences, a fluid motion of laughter, tears, passions, joys, and the ever-present knowledge of what God has done for me. God is always our friend. He loves us, no matter what we do to upset Him. God gave us the innate ability to invest wisely to solve our own problems, seek out unfamiliar definitions of happiness, and so much more.

I was recently pondering all this at my birthplace in Northport. The kids still run and play. The houses next to where I spent hours falling on my old walking platform are long gone. The cleared lots remind me of progress that has taken place in my old neighborhood. Many children who played around me in my youth are in jail, some are dead, but a few own successful businesses or have gone on to professional careers after completing a college education. The dirt road is paved and most of the elder members of the community have gone on.

A new generation, full of undetermined promise and laden with opportunity, has taken the reins from our past to complete the cycle of life. The shotgun house my family once rented is basically the same. All that remains of our old cherry tree is a rotted-out stump. Uncle Nora and I talked away hours under that fateful tree discussing my role in the arena of life. I have often contemplated how my life would have unfolded without such a stable male role model, but only lately have I begun to wonder what life for Uncle Nora would have been like without me. Supposing that were true, something recently struck a chord in me.

He would say, "Son, people are going to try to tell you what you can't do because you are in dat chair, but Nate, I done tol' you dat God put you in dat chair for a reason." Nora noticed something that everybody but he and Auntie missed. What he saw was a drive in me much like his own. Nurtured, it could become the formal education that was missing from his life, and neither Annie Bell nor Uncle Nora were going to let my education pass them by. That is why he pushed me like he did.

Nora was saying to himself all that time, "I have a chance at fulfilling my dreams through this boy." I never completely understood until now that, hidden inside his gentle encouragement and urgent pleas over the years, there lay an unspoken promise to himself. He was freeing himself from a limited sense of personal success through my success. The world had said, "No!" to his entire generation's plea for equality. Struggling for their civil rights, Nora and his peers had been written off by American society as little more than tools of the military and the service industry.

He knew, despite all the labels I would receive throughout my life such as "uneducable mentally retarded," I was a living anomaly: a monkey wrench in the gears of pigeonhole testing, labeling, and academic tracking of children in public education. Uncle Nora surmised long ago that, to the world beyond Northport, Alabama, I could grow into a dangerous young man. A severely underpriviledged and disabled black man of ability and acheivement stood in stark contrast to all the writing-off of future generations of children from similar circumstances. His many summertime lessons, learned under the shade of my childhood cherry tree, were geared toward numbing me to criticism of my efforts to acheive. Those simple chats, between sips of lemonade, gradually equipped me to fuel my ongoing revolution.

Epilogue

As I rest overlooking the water, the waves wash the shore in both directions, and I am reminded of what Nora said: "You can make it if you try." My friends have helped in many ways to realize a dream that has taken me to various parts of the country and into the depths of my very soul over the course of twenty years. I am whole and free. I am one with myself.

Children play in the nearby surf, reminding me of my own youth and of the infinite possibilities of childhood. The future lies with change, and change lies with understanding, reaching out toward and encouraging all of our youth. My vision of our potential is unlimited, as is the salt in the sea, more pressing than the draw of the tide. This is no time for turning back.

I cannot do justice to the ocean shore, something so spiritual, compelling, powerfully humbling. Each wave represents a new opportunity, another suggestion, receiving continuous motivation from an undiscovered source. She is speaking to me now, in my second trip to greet her: "You have been blessed with many gifts. Your brother and uncle thank you for sharing them with so many people. This is your time now." It is my time, but it is ours as well.

Momma recently exclaimed, "Lord, don't move the mountain, just give me the strength to climb it." In writing this story, I have conquered many obstacles, but the biggest has been fear of self. There are many dream killers besides fear. Greed, pride, hatred, and ignorance are large and sometimes curiously self-inflicted obstacles to social change. Some patience, recognition of imperfection, understanding, and respect—for each other, the natural environment, and global community—would go a long way toward progress in a good direction for our country.

Families are our greatest treasures. Every background, creed, and religion, most all of which are represented in America in one form or another, has a history that we should all share, be educated in, and be respectful of. Without family values we lose families. Without families we die.

I know that God put me together with many others for a specific purpose. Despite our differences, we have all the means necessary to remain on the course which is mapped out before me in patterns of the sea. I have struggled financially for quite some time, but I am at peace. No possession except of yourself and God will bring you wealth or happiness. It takes some people a lifetime to learn this; others never do.

Education starts at home, accelerates in school and continues throughout life. I value my education more than anything else. One experience in particular, writing my name on paper in two languages, holds more meaning for me now than writing my entire life story. In learning to print my name, I have written my life story. I am an educated man.

I was illiterate until my twenty-first year of life, but today I speak three languages. Illiteracy is a disease that plagues many, within the disabled community and without. As long as one person is illiterate, the epidemic remains. If you can read, imagine what it must be like for those uneducated people who cannot share in that gift, though they can share a great deal more. Illiteracy is a silent dream killer, but it doesn't imply ignorance. Life is itself a teacher, and its students teach the lessons of their experience.

I met Gil Scott-Heron in Birmingham on May 18, 1995, and exchanged a few words. He, my friends in the Dave Matthews Band and many others I have known, would agree that countless undiscovered artists speak through the discovery of their individual mosaics. I encourage you to find your own. As long as you waste your gifts, you have a severe handicap. If you fail to constantly develop a perspective, you have a disability. If you fit into neither category, then you, too, are free. I know I can speak for my uncle in saying, "Believing in your dreams, regardless of others' opinions, is the first and last step toward success."

"Recess is over!" I am smitten with sanctimonious people lacking vision telling me how things should be. It's time for each of us to find ways of coaching the game, because we all share power to shape the rules together. If you've been mistreated or somehow wronged by a criminal, don't let anger blind your perception of your assailant's humanity. Even hardened delinquents can learn and find ways to contribute to society if they are forgiven for past mistakes, and shown how to be a citizen by example.

The power that we share is the love of God, which has often been misrepresented by sinners within the Christian faith throughout history. I have overcome many obstacles which you may experience one or two of in your entire lifetime. This is the book of my experience. Experience has taught me not to close my mind to the changing nature of truth, and to remember who determines what I can accomplish. As Michael Jordan would say, "The ball is in your court now."

The last and most important thing I would like to say is, with God in your life, anything is possible. He is up there, don't be fooled; and He does answer prayers according to His own designs. My gift to you comes undeniably through His intervention. The coincidences abound to the point where coincidences cease and miracles begin. As I sit, overlooking the water, the exuberant future for civilization remains bountiful and endless.

NATHAN BALLARD

Index

N

O

P

T

U